Not By Bread Alone

memoir of a jurist

Delilah Vidallon-Magtolis
2012

Dedication

To my dear husband Isagani, and daughters Gail, Joy and Grace, whose steadfast love, unstinted support and understanding of the rigors of my judicial duties through all the years I served as a jurist, have inspired me to write this memoir; as well as to my grandchildren, Zachary and Azrielle, who provided fresh inspiration during the last few years of my judicial service.

Acknowledgment

*M*uch thanks and appreciation are due to my daughter Grace who painstakingly edited the manuscript despite her heavy workload both in office and in church; to Ms. Leticia Javier of the Supreme Court Printing Office for her technical assistance in the printing of this memoir; and to my son-in-law, Bobby Alguso who designed the cover page.

Foreword

When I was a trial judge, some of my friends would come to me to report on alleged misdeeds of fellow judges or court personnel. I defended them to the hilt. I dismissed the reports as character assassination. I used to say an emphatic "NO," that story cannot be true, for we judges do what is right, and act according to what we know to be the law as applied to the facts before us. Sometime later, when I came face to face with real hard facts, I had to eat my words in shame.

Indeed, there are colleagues who should rightfully be called "HOODLUMS IN ROBES," as one former President described judges. The nature of the duties and responsibilities of judges make them susceptible to temptations which are often so strong.

Perhaps it is because of the low pay of judges then. When I first entered the judiciary as a judge of the first level court (Metropolitan Trial Court of Quezon City) in 1983, the monthly salary of judges of the first level courts was only P5,700. Even with the allowance given by the City Government in the amount of P3,000 per month, the total is still much lower than the income of an average lawyer. But, should that be an excuse? I think not.

After all, men should not live by bread alone, but every word that comes from God, as admonished by Jesus Christ when he was tempted by the devil. If they succumbed to the temptation, then Satan would be clapping his hands in victory.

This is a collection of experiences to show all and sundry how to uphold the majesty of the law despite the lure of easy money or get-rich-quick syndromes; how to resist pressure; how to overcome fear; how to temper justice with mercy; how to keep friendship without succumbing to unjust demands; and how to stand upright against the easy wrong.

Above all, it is a testimony to how God's grace has sustained me in the endless contest of right against wrong and to live by faith in His provision and perfect plan.

Table of Contents

Not by Bread Alone
Memoir of a Jurist

ᝏ ᝏ

The Years Before

THE RELUCTANT LAWYER

"No, Ma'am. I will never be a lawyer. Because lawyers are liars."

Such was my curt reply to my History teacher in fourth year high school, when she told me that I should be a lawyer because I could allegedly discuss my answers to her questions very well.

I do not know how I got that idea about lawyers. In any case, becoming a lawyer was never my dream.

Since I was a child, my ambition had always been to be a doctor. Maybe it was because I was very sickly as an infant up to my pre-school years, and I wanted to know why I suffered so much from convulsions whenever I had fever. As far back as I could remember, I felt like falling down deep crevices, or being rolled over by big rocks, or being chased by some wild supernatural beings. I dreaded those nightmares during convulsions, making me cling to my mother (Mumsy) in fear during such illnesses. This made one doctor who attended me to remark that perhaps I was going crazy — prompting Mumsy to avoid that doctor forever.

1

THE FRUSTRATED PHYSICIAN

As I was growing up, however, it became obvious that I could never be a doctor. First, the sight of fresh blood makes me feel nauseated. I fainted when I watched my brother, Kuya Sanny, as he underwent a tonsillectomy. His nurses-friends with whom I so bravely entered the observation deck of the operating room had to take me out so that I could lie down and be given medication until I recovered.

I also fainted when I, like a big sister, courageously and voluntarily accompanied my sister Leddy to the dentist to have her tooth extracted. I was standing beside her, holding her hand while the dentist was slowly boring holes around her tooth. Turning around to avoid seeing the oozing blood from her gums, I suddenly lost consciousness and fell to the floor, making the dentist attending her to be so nervous that she had to call a male colleague to continue the extraction process.

The other reason I knew why I could not be a doctor was poverty. My father (Dadsy) was a protestant pastor, while Mumsy was a public school teacher who never returned to teaching after the Second World War, although she was a Model Teacher in pre-war years and was selected to be government *pensionada* to the United States of America (USA), which she waived to take care of her family. Like many other families that time, we had no housemaid or helper.

HUMBLE BEGINNINGS

Protestant pastors in the Philippines are so poorly paid. In fact, I learned that when the government fixed the minimum salary of government employees at P120 per month, Dadsy was receiving only P30 monthly from the rural church he was serving. This was only augmented by Dadsy's occasional earnings through selling insurance policies. And by God's grace, all our needs were supplied.

Mumsy was very good at budgeting and managing the household at minimal cost. She could cook all sorts of Filipino dishes, provide for our basic needs, and still save some money for rainy days. Sometimes, I used to wonder why there were only three fried eggs on our breakfast table when there were six of us in the family. This meant we had to share an egg with another. This way, we learned to share whatever we had with others.

Living within our means while sharing our blessings with others was part of our way of life. No appeal for help by needy families was turned down. Children of provincial pastors sent their children to live with us in Manila — with free board and lodging —- so that they could pursue their studies in the city. And whenever the parents came to visit their children, they also stayed with us at home for quite some time.

There was in fact a time when three young men, Bert, Ben and Vic (Norberto Dilag of Amadeo, Cavite; Benjamin de la Peña of Bailen, Cavite; and Vicente Alvarez of Libmanan, Camarines Sur) were living with us all at the same time, the condition being that they help in cleaning the house and washing the dishes. All three finished college: Bert became a Certified Public Accountant (CPA) and bank executive, Ben became a pastor, and Vic was a rare graduate of Fish Technology and a highly paid technocrat.

Mumsy also sewed all the dresses for myself and my two sisters. She had a *suki* in Divisoria, from whom she bought *retasos* by the kilo which she made into dresses. Sometimes, she used as dress materials the washed sacks of chicken feeds which had colorful designs. She even sewed all our attires for special occasions, such as birthdays, graduations, proms, and even our wedding gowns as well as those of our entire bridal entourage. Thus, I never learned to choose my own clothes, and just wore whatever Mumsy sewed and provided. It was only when I was already a judge, and she had gone to the Great Beyond that I was forced to buy RTW dresses and other garments from stores.

Another little known fact about my family is that my siblings and I are all products of public schools. Kuya Sanny and I studied at Lakandula Elementary School in Tondo, Manila, which was more than three (3) kilometers from our house, located near the boundary of Manila and Caloocan. Our two younger sisters, Leddy and Nievy, were more fortunate, because their elementary school was closer to our house.

Kuya Sanny and I walked all the way to and from Lakandula, through swampy roads and railroad tracks, and crossed over creeks which would swell into rivers during rainy days. We also walked to the house of our piano teacher in Dimasalang, Sampaloc, Manila, which was also about 3-4 kilometers from our residence.

We also had schedules for cleaning the house and washing the dishes. We helped in other household chores whenever within our capability.

All these notwithstanding, we have fond memories of our happy childhood. We were a happy, loving family. We enjoyed our togetherness, especially in going to church or singing at home, or just being together. Our parents inculcated in us the basic Christian values, disciplined us with love, and made sure we got the best education they could afford. With God's help, we attained not only basic college education but post graduate studies as well.

STORMS THRU THE EDUCATIONAL LADDER

To make up for lost time during the war years, Kuya Sanny and I enrolled in summer classes and finished high school in three years.

It was during my high school days that an unscrupulous American couple took advantage of Dadsy and Mumsy. Dadsy first met the husband (Jack) while he was promoting his insurance undertaking. The guy appeared to be impoverished and needed help. Dadsy brought him home for lunch and for more meals afterwards.

Later, Jack brought his wife Janet too. They were in and out of our house for meals and overnight stay whenever they were in the city, although Janet usually stayed in Baguio purportedly to attend to the court case of her father whose estate was allegedly locked in a long court battle. According to Janet, she was the lone heiress to a mine field, and she was represented in the case by a famous lawyer, Atty. Jose W. Diokno (who later became a Senator), but there were huge expenditures to meet in the meantime.

Janet oftentimes called us to listen while she used our phone to dial a number, asking for Atty. Diokno. Without our hearing what the person at the other end of the line was saying, she would pass on to us the "reassurances" of Atty. Diokno that they were winning the case whose end was in sight, although more and more expenses had to be met in the meantime.

They then started their borrowing of funds from Mumsy to finance the costly court case. To protect Mumsy, Janet asked another prominent lawyer (Atty. Neptali Gonzales who also became a Senator) to draw a Last Will and Testament, signed by her, making Mumsy the administrator of her estate in case anything happened to her.

Mumsy lent her savings little by little, until they were dissipated. After that, Dadsy and Mumsy had to mortgage the properties they had acquired through Mumsy's savings one after another, as well as our residential house and lot. Our well-to-do neighbors were just too willing to lend their funds upon the guarantee of Mumsy, who was a respected and prominent socio-civic leader in the community.

After a year or so of the spouses' living in my parents' misplaced generosity, the couple fled to the USA with only a short letter to Mumsy saying that they will return to pay their debts. Of course they never did.

Mumsy had nervous breakdowns and was in and out of the hospital after that. She was so ashamed of herself not only for having trusted an unworthy couple but also for having dragged our neighbors to also lend money. Without planning to redeem their mortgaged properties, Dadsy and Mumsy decided to leave our family home. They bought the right to a small restaurant at the Rotonda of Sta. Mesa and transferred our family there to live at the second floor of the restaurant.

Mumsy took it upon herself to be the chief cook, marketer and manager of the restaurant. She would wake up very early every morning (except Sundays, when the restaurant was closed) to buy the supplies needed for the restaurant. This kept her busy, and she got over her nervousness and despondency. I helped in the family business by washing dishes, waiting on tables, and getting orders and delivering packed lunch to employees of nearby offices, mostly the Bureau of Census and Statistics, now the National Statistics Office (NSO). I also issued receipts and kept the books of account for the restaurant. Leddy and Nievy were still young and in elementary school at that time.

AT THE CROSSROADS

After graduating from high school, I was at the crossroads, not knowing what short course to take in order to help Dadsy and Mumsy from the quagmire they had fallen into. I enrolled first at the Philippine Christian College (now Philippine Christian University) for a general course leading towards a Bachelor of Arts degree. But I was confused as to what I should do after graduating. Teach? No way. That was the profession abandoned by Mumsy. Besides, the sight of test tubes and chemical formulae in my Chemistry class so intimidated me that I decided to drop the subject.

The idea of becoming a banker came flashing by. I thus transferred to the Far Eastern University (FEU) to take up Commerce, major in Banking and Finance. I earned my degree in Commerce in three years by enrolling in evening classes and through all summers so that I could still help in the family business.

Armed with a Bachelor of Science in Commerce degree, I immediately went to several banks to seek employment. Unfortunately, although I was passing their pre-employment examinations, my young age hindered my hiring. I was 19 then, but they wanted someone at least 21 years old.

It was in one of such frustrating days that I came home to find Dadsy opening a full-page advertisement in the Manila Times (the leading news daily then) of Francisco College (formerly , Francisco Law School), announcing the availability of scholarships in the College of Law to those who will pass their scholarship examination. Dadsy encouraged me to go. My protests were countered by his saying, *"Wala ka naming ginagawa."* That challenged me to go.

I arrived at Francisco College on the day of the examination. When I read the requirements, I learned that I was not qualified. Not having taken the pre-law course, I had no credited units in Political Science, and was deficient in the required units in English, Spanish and Mathematics. I was returning the papers, but the Dean (Prof. Jose P. Bengzon, who later became a Justice of the Court of Appeals and later also of the Supreme Court) told me to stay on and take the test, since there was nothing to lose anyway. I did, and miraculously passed the scholarship examination.

Thus, my becoming a lawyer was the result of an accident and of necessity: the accident was my passing a scholarship examination in law without being qualified nor prepared to take it, and the necessity was the need for a family lawyer to protect its members from unscrupulous people who take advantage of the innocent for their own selfish interests.

But was it really accidental? On hindsight, it was God's leading. For how else could I have answered the Political Science questions from what I learned in Philippine History and

Government in high school? And how did my high school background in General Mathematics, Algebra and Geometry come handy to help me answer the questions in Advanced Mathematics? English was easy; it has always been my favorite subject. But Spanish? *Por Pavor!* God indeed works in mysterious ways.

CHALLENGES AND CONCERNS IN LAW SCHOOL

Having learned from our regular customers in our family restaurant that there was going to be an examination for prospective casual employees at the then Bureau of Census and Statistics, which was three blocks away from our residence/ restaurant, I took and passed the competitive examination. I was hired as a casual clerk for a project in Demography in partnership with the National Economic Council (now, the National Economic Development Authority or NEDA). I was thus a working student in government in the first two years of my law studies. When my casual employment was terminated due to completion of the project, I resumed my work in the family-operated restaurant.

My scholarship only covered my tuition fees and did not include miscellaneous expenses and books. I could only provide myself with copies of the codified laws without commentaries or explanations (more popularly known as "Codes" in law school parlance), which I studied during my rides to school. Before and after classes, while in school, I usually stayed in the library to read the textbooks and assigned cases. A columnist in our school newspaper noticed this, so he wrote in his column one day: *"Scholar Delilah Vidallon lives in the library."*

At this point, Kuya Sanny had become employed and he decided to defray my school allowance of P10 per month or P5.00 every two weeks. This amounted to fifty centavos every school day, Monday thru Friday. Forty centavos was used for fare, since I had to take two jeepney rides at P0.10 each in going to and from school. This left me only ten centavos for snacks, with which I could only buy a bottle of soft drink, as sandwiches and pastries cost more. But I detested carbonated drinks, so I took snacks only every other day, indulging in my weakness, ice cream. Back then, Pacosta Ice Cream retailed at P0.20 per serving brick, and I relished being able to afford it every other day.

On my second year in law school, there was a professor (Atty. Abraham F. Sarmiento who also became a Supreme Court Justice) who so intimidated me because I got a low grade in our mid-term exam in the Civil Law on Property. He announced to the class: *"It is a pity that our scholar did not live up to expectations"*. He gave me my lowest grade ever (83%) in my entire law studies. I wanted to quit then, but our Dean told me to stay.

Upon knowing of my lack of books, our Dean kindly called the publisher of the books authored by our College President, former Senator Vicente Francisco, and ordered books for me for the major subjects used during the second semester of my 2nd year. He then asked me to enroll right then and there. Those were the very first law books I ever owned.

It was a good thing that my graded average enabled me to still maintain my scholarship. So I enrolled again, and again, until I earned my law degree.

Fortunately, I was able to redeem myself during my 4th year in law school, when I could not avoid Prof. Sarmiento because he alone was handling Civil Law Review. This time, he gave me 95% --- the highest possible grade in law school.

When we later met after I had become a full-fledged lawyer, he introduced me to his friends as "my former student, and a very bright one."

My free law books were later augmented during our graduation. When I graduated at the top of my class, I was awarded two other law books, aside from two gold medals, the first for being *Class Valedictorian,* and the other for having written the *Best Thesis.* These books comprised my entire law library at home during my entire student life and beyond — truly the perfect graduation gift.

Pre-judicial Service

Chapter 2

EARLY STINT IN GOVERNMENT

After passing the Bar Exams and a week after I took my oath as a lawyer, I was recalled by the Bureau of Census and Statistics for regular employment. Although the position given me was that of Clerical Aide, the lowest clerical position in the Civil Service and a very demeaning position for a lawyer, the following factors weighed heavily in favor of my acceptance: first, the office is located very near our residence, such that I would be saving on lunch and transportation money; second, it was a sure employment for someone who did not intend to practice law, and would spare me the ignominy of going through applying for a position from office to office again; and third, I could still help in our restaurant business.

I thus graciously accepted the position and promptly gave half of my salary to Mumsy to help in the family expenses.

Without my seeking or working for promotion, I was pushed for promotion by my supervisors as early as a few months after my employment, and gradually rose through the ranks from clerical through statistical, then legal positions until I reached the second highest position in the Office of the Civil Registrar General (OCRG). Here, my immediate boss who was then in his senior years, gave me a free hand to work on the improvement of the OCRG. I then devised the forms used for certifications, endorsements, and other documents needed or used in the office, and made recommendations to streamline the operations of the OCRG, which is the general repository of all records of births, deaths, marriages, and documents pertaining to citizenship.

JUDICIAL EXPOSURE

It was while occupying the position of Assistant Civil Registry Officer (Assistant Chief of Division) that I was plucked by then Judge Corazon Juliano Agrava to work with her at the Juvenile and Domestic Relations Court of Manila (JDRC). Impressed by my academic background, including post-graduate units in Public Administration which I earned as a scholar (again, after a competitive examination) in the University of the Philippines, Judge Agrava made me a Hearing Office and Deputy Clerk of Court, concurrently her Personnel Officer in the JDRC of Manila.

My work in the JDRC exposed me to courtroom trial. I also learned how to conduct hearings in non-controversial special proceedings. Sometimes, Judge Agrava appointed me as a representative of the State, in lieu a Solicitor from the Office of the Solicitor General (OSG), to cross examine the petitioners' witnesses and see to it that the evidence is not fabricated.

The door opened for me to be employed at the Supreme Court when my former Dean and Professor, Justice Jose P. Bengzon, discovered that I was at the JDRC of Manila. Judge Agrava brought me to a Judges' affair to accompany at the piano their guest singer, Diomedes Maturan, then popularly known as the Perry Como of the Philippines. Since I could play the piano by ear, I accompanied his singing of his signature song plus an encore number. The affair was attended by Justice Bengzon, and he sought me after the musical numbers. It turned out that Justice Bengzon had been looking for me since I passed the Bar, but I never got his message.

Justice Bengzon asked me to see the Clerk of Court of the Supreme Court (SC) at the time, Atty. Romeo D. Mendoza, the following Monday. After an instant examination given by the SC Chief Attorney which I surprisingly passed, Atty. Mendoza immediately took me in as a Court Attorney in his staff, to the consternation of Judge Agrava who tearfully tried to convince me not to leave, but she eventually let me go.

At the SC Office of the Clerk of Court, I became known as the 'Bionic Woman' because the assignments given by Atty. Mendoza were expeditiously disposed of, such that the backlog of administrative cases piled as tall as myself in his office were terminated in record time, and assignments from some of the SC Justices which usually were "rush" were given to me and accomplished before the stated deadline.

Justice Felix V. Makasiar, one of the SC's Associate Justices, usually asks Atty. Mendoza for lawyers' assistance in some of his special assignments. I was one of those "lent" by Atty. Mendoza to the Justice. The latter was apparently impressed with my work, such that the next thing I knew, he asked that I be transferred to his office. While working for and with Justice Makasiar, the Judiciary Reorganization Act took effect in January 1983.

AN UNEXPECTED APPOINTMENT

As a first step to the judiciary reorganization, all judges were considered resigned and were to be evaluated by the Integrity Council created by then President Marcos. To attract new applicants for judicial positions, the Integrity Council and the Department of Justice (DOJ) conducted a Judiciary Reorganization Seminar (JURIS) for prospective appointees.

Justice Makasiar sent all lawyers in his staff to enroll in JURIS. There were two exams given in the JURIS, before and after the actual 2-week training. I was to learn later that I passed the exams, and was first recommended to be a Regional Trial Court (RTC) judge in Ilagan, Isabela, but was objected to by the Regional Chairman of the Kilusang Bagong Lipunan (KBL), the dominant political party at that time. Later, the Integrity Council recommended me to the RTC of Bayambang, Nueva Vizcaya, but was again objected to by a high-ranking officer of the KBL.

The objections of both Members of Parliament or *Mambabatas Pambansa* (MP) were allegedly because they did not know me. Silently, I thanked them for their objections, knowing that I did not want to be uprooted from my family if ever I became a judge.

Some well-meaning friends urged me to go and see the objecting MPs, or go directly to the then Speaker of the *Batasang Pambansa* who was a former Justice of the Supreme Court, Hon. Querube Makalintal. But I declined, reasoning out that I was not sure if I wanted to be a judge, and I certainly would not accept the appointment if I was assigned to a distant province.

Wonder of all wonders, I was nominated again by the Integrity Council to the Metropolitan Trial Court (MeTC) of Quezon City. More surprising was that no one objected to this nomination; hence, I was eventually appointed as such. The MeTC is a first level court, which is one notch lower than the RTC. But the salary difference was only P1,000. This is more than made up for by the allowance given by the City Government of Quezon City to its judges. What is more, an appointment to the National Capital Judicial Region is considered as a plum assignment and difficult to get.

I could not believe how things turned out until the former Court Administrator, Justice Leo Medialdea, called me to deliver a copy of my appointment. After noting that I resided in Quezon City, he remarked as he was handing me my appointment papers: *"Ikaw pala Delilah ay parang pagong na itinapon sa tubig"*. Such statement is a confirmation of the news I got that I was first nominated to two distant courts which met with objections. The Quezon City courts are located just 15 minutes away from our house.

What an unexpected blessing!

When we took our oath as judges, several people, after congratulating me, asked in jest, *"Ang lakas mo. Sino ang backer mo?"* They did not believe that I had none. But on second thought, I did have a Backer, the most powerful any person could have. And apparently, God was not done with me yet.

☙ ❧

Birthing Pains

INITIAL PROBLEMS

When I was appointed as Presiding Judge of Branch 41 of the MeTC of Quezon City, my first problem was space. The Quezon City government could not immediately provide sufficient rooms for the newly created Court branches in the said city. I had to initially share the office space and courtroom of another judge, Judge Nestor Batungbacal, who let me use the room of his Branch Clerk of Court as my office, and we alternated in using his courtroom for our trials. This arrangement helped fill my need for court personnel during trials, because his staff could assist in my conduct of hearings while the recruitment, selection and appointment of my own staff were in process.

My next problem was the court staff. Although I was appointed to a new branch of the MeTC, we were directed by the Office of the Court Administrator (OCA) of the Supreme Court to absorb the court personnel of the former City Courts which were abolished through the judiciary reorganization. I had wanted to select all members of my own staff so that I could be sure of their integrity, but I was forced to fill five (5) out of eleven (11) positions in my staff with former employees of the abolished City Courts.

So in my first conference with my staff, I inculcated in them my requirement for honesty and integrity. I told them I could forgive their occasional errors and lapses in their work, but not any form of dishonesty. I told them that if they committed honest mistakes, I would defend them to the hilt, but if they committed any form of dishonesty, I would even be the one to prosecute them.

The third problem was tardiness. The old employees whom I absorbed were prone to coming late to the office, sometimes even later than 9:00 A.M. when office hours started at 8:00 A.M. When I called them to a conference about the importance of coming to office promptly, so that I could also start my court sessions at 8:30 A.M. as mandated by the Supreme Court, I found that some live in distant places like Macabebe, Pampanga, such that their habitual tardiness was tolerated by their former judge. No wonder, some judges started their court sessions about 10:00 A.M. or even later.

I then appealed to my staff to help me start court sessions promptly at 8:30 A.M. I told them to sign our logbook of attendance, which I shall close with a red demarcation with my signature, and those signing up after the demarcation line will be accordingly considered to have come in late. Knowing that old habits are difficult to break, I told them that I shall do it gradually, such that the demarcation line shall be at 9:00 A.M. on the first week, at 8:45 on the second week, at 8:30 on the third week, and at 8:15 on the fourth week. Before the first week was over, all my staff members were arriving before 8:00 A.M. My demarcation line was moved to 8:25 A.M., just a few minutes before the start of court sessions. I was happy to be able to bang my gavel (to indicate the start of court sessions) promptly at 8:30 A.M.

Finally, and most importantly, I inherited a heavy caseload. Although I was appointed to a new court branch, it did not mean that I would tackle only newly filed cases. On the contrary, I inherited about 2,000 cases, most of which were already submitted (ripe) for decision and were left unresolved by other judges of the former City Court. I thus directed an inventory of all cases assigned to me, made index cards for each of them, and sorted them according to age, so that I could prioritize those that have been lying idle for a long time, starting from the oldest.

I used half of my official time in deciding cases already submitted for decision, oftentimes even bringing home case records to be able to work on them in the evenings.

After initially tackling the above problems, I issued these ground rules for my staff to follow:

1. All employees must come promptly at 8:00A.M., as I will bang the gavel for court sessions exactly at 8:30 A.M.

2. The employees on duty in the courtroom, *i.e.* the Branch Clerk of Court, the Court Interpreter, the Stenographer on duty, and the Court Bailiff shall be in their proper places inside the courtroom not later than 8:25 A.M.

3. Case records for hearing should be on my desk one day before the hearing.

4. No employee is allowed to receive any kind of gift or present for me.

5. No party litigant or counsel shall be allowed inside my chambers, unless accompanied by the adverse party or its counsel.

6. No employee shall receive anything from a party litigant or counsel in consideration of any case.

7. All judgments, resolutions and orders shall be released promptly within 24 hours from promulgation or signing.

8. No employee shall intercede for any party with pending cases.

9. Any form of dishonesty shall be administratively dealt with.

10. All employees shall render prompt, courteous and honest service.

FIRST BRUSH

Because I still lacked a Court Bailiff, AA, the bailiff of Judge Batungbakal volunteered his services. I appreciated his offer, which enabled me to hold sessions even as half of the positions in my staff complement were still unfilled.

One day after trial, I noticed through the glass wall of my temporary office, a certain guy talking to Bailiff AA, apparently agitated. He came back the next day and the next. Looking at AA, he seemed to be saying something to the guy in an angry manner. I called both of them to my chambers to ask what the matter was. The guy said that he has been coming to collect the refund of his bailbond because his case had already been dismissed. But Bailiff AA cut him short, saying that his bailbond had already been refunded, showing a note on the cover of the case record. I asked to see the note and found the following handwritten on the cover: "Bailbond refunded, per receipt No. ____." It was dated and initialed by somebody. While I was reading, I noticed that AA was trying to reach the foot of the guy with his right foot.

"*Ma'am, hindi pa po ako nababayaran,*"uttered the guy.

"*Nabayaran ka na!*", retorted AA in a menacing tone, at the same time kicking the guy's foot.

"*Hindi pa po, Ma'am. Pinababalik-balik niya po ako,*" answered the guy and began to cry.

"*Maawa ka naman sa 'kin. Inutang ko lang yan...*"

"*Sino ba'ang nagsulat nito?*" I asked AA, pointing to the remarks at the case cover. .

"Sa Clerk of Court po."

"Okay. I'll have this investigated. You better tell the truth, AA, or I'll have you administratively charged."

Suddenly, AA's face softened as he confessed: *"Sorry po, Judge, nagipit lang po ako."*

"So, pay him not later than tomorrow. And don't ever do that again."

"Yes, Ma'am. Judge, hinihiling ko lang po, huwag na niyong paratingin ito okay Judge Batungbakal." (The judge happened to be on extended leave then.)

"Okay, kung hindi ka na uulit... Magmula ngayon, huwag ka nang makikialam sa mga kaso ko. Hindi ka na mag-du-duty sa mga hearings ko. At huwag kang maka-hawak-hawak ng mga case records ko."

"Opo, ma'am."

The following day, I called our Executive Judge (EJ) to report on what happened, and to ask him to investigate if there is connivance with AA and any staff of the Office of the Clerk of Court which is under his direct supervision, in contrast to the Branch Clerk of Court of each and every judge, which is directly supervised by the latter.

In response, EJ called me for a meeting with the staff of the Clerk of Court. When I arrived, EJ informed them about my report. He asked them one by one whether there is a syndicate operating within the office of the Clerk of Court in connivance with personnel of any branch to deprive acquitted accused of the lawful refund of their bailbonds. One by one, the staff answered, "none, sir."

"O, wala daw," EJ declared. The meeting was adjourned, without the EJ's even finding out who wrote the remarks on the cover of the case record.

From then on, I knew that I will fight my own battles against corruption and only within my own sala. I became doubly cautious about hiring the rest of my staff. Aside from the required NBI and Police clearances, I also referred the applicants to Dr. Cecilia Villegas a friend-psychiatrist, for a psychological and psychiatric evaluation to check on their attitudes and moral outlook in life.   I also prayed a lot for guidance in hiring my court staff. Fortunately, after clearance from Dr. Villegas, those I selected for appointment proved to be efficient and trustworthy.

STAFF EXTRAS

Whenever a lawyer or party-litigant asks for a copy of any portion of the records of a case, the photo-copying has to be done outside, since we have no Xerox or copying machine in the office. But the records cannot be brought out except by a member of my staff, who is directed to accompany the interested party, carry and guard the records and show me afterwards what was copied and that the original is still there.

Once, I saw my driver after returning with case records, apparently with money in his polo pocket. "Ano yan? Binayaran ka ba ng abogado?"

"Ma'am, ayaw ko sanang tanggapin pero pinilit po ako. Nilagay nga sa bulsa ko."

"Sinabi ko na sa inyo, huag kayong tatanggap ng anumang amount o regalo buhat sa mga taong may kaso dito."

"Ma'am, ngayon lang po nangyari to. At saka maliit lang. Sukli lang po naman."

I called all the members of my staff and reminded them against receiving any amount of money or gifts from party litigants or lawyers. "If there is a first time, there will surely be a second, and a third, and so on, basta nakakalusot. Magsimula kayo ng maliit ngayon, bukas o sa makalawa, lalaki na ng lalaki iyan. Magiging habit na nyo yan. Alam ba niyo, ang tinaggap niyo ngayon, bukas ubos na yan. Ang hindi mauubos ang magandang pangalan. Ang magandang reputation ninyo at ng branch na ito, yan ang hindi kukupas."

In addition, I also directed my staff not to receive any gift intended for me from any lawyer or party with pending cases, or any amount – big or small, except complimentary give-aways by companies during Christmas, such as calendars or diaries, which are given to all and not to any particular judge.

UNAUTHORIZED FEES AND COMMISSIONS

Sometime later, I got a tip that one of my stenographers was collecting marriage fees — supposedly for me — from parties whose marriage I solemnized, although I never charge for such services because I consider it a public service since the same is performed in my chambers or in the courtroom during office hours.

There's also a clerk who waylays people charged with criminal offenses and refers them to certain sureties or bonding companies — for which she got commissions. Bailbonds issued by surety companies are not always acceptable to the courts and run the risk of disapproval because of pending obligations that remain unpaid. The selection of bonding companies is supposed to be by raffle among qualified bonding companies.

After I talked to them, the clerk promised to refrain from dealing with bonding companies, while the stenographer asked permission to transfer to another branch of the RTC in Quezon City – which I willingly gave. In less than one year, the stenographer visited me at my office and said that her new boss-judge issues TROs (temporary restraining orders) indiscriminately for a price in four or five digits, depending on the financial status of the applicant. Injunctions are priced higher. It was from her that I learned the term "envelopmental justice"

No wonder the said judge celebrates his birthdays with lavish feasts and unending streams of visitors, with no less than twenty lechons and bottomless pit of wines. But the sumptuous parties ended after the judge was dismissed from the service for accepting a Pajero and a substantial amount from a litigant.

Maintaining Independence

WHEN OTHERS INTERCEDE

One of my biggest challenges as a judge is how to maintain independence even when high-ranking officials or even fellow judges call on me to intercede for a party on a case. Among those who have called me to ask for favorable resolutions on certain cases were a Secretary of Justice, a Congressman, and higher judicial officials. My standard answer was that I will study the case mentioned very carefully, but I never promised on how I would resolve the cases they were interested in. One or two of my former colleagues who were promoted to higher courts never talked to me afterwards when I did not decide the case for which they interceded according to their wishes.

A Congressman even visited me personally in connection with a case. I do not remember the name of the congressman or even the docket number of the case he was interested in, because I took note of the case number on a small piece of paper, as I usually did, then discarded it afterwards. Naturally, I do not even remember how the case was decided, but I was certain that I decided the case fairly according to the evidence.

INQUIRIES FROM COLLEAGUES

"Lily, is it true that you do not admit people with cases in your chambers?"

It was Judge C, a fellow judge of the RTC of Quezon City, then the national president of the Philippine Judges Association (PJA), who was at the phone at the time.

"Yes," I answered. *"I avoid seeing lawyers and party litigants with pending cases in the privacy of my chambers unless they are accompanied by the adverse party or counsel. This is to avoid any suspicion that there was an under-the-table deal, or that an offer for such was made in consideration of their case."*

"How about me, are you not going to admit me?" he asked.

"Oh, you are welcome anytime. That rule only applies to lawyers and people with cases. But not to my colleagues."

Within five minutes, Judge C was in my chambers. He was interceding for Ms. L, a woman who was claiming a share in the estate of a deceased person whose intestate case was pending before me. As usual, I promised to study her claim very carefully, without any commitment on how I will resolve it.

It turned out that Ms. L was a former live-in partner of the deceased. Since she had no legal relationship with said deceased, and she did not present any proof that she contributed to the acquisition of any property of the deceased, I had to deny her claim. In fairness to Judge C, he never called back to question my resolution.

A year or so thereafter, a front page news in a major daily reported that Judge C, the incumbent PJA president, was dismissed from the service for immorality. After due investigation by a committee created by the Supreme Court, Judge C was found to be living with Ms. L, whom he had housed in an apartment and with whom he had sired a baby, while still being married to a woman from a prominent family. A staff in his office testified that he had been doing errands at the behest of Judge C for Ms. L before and after she gave birth and for many more times afterwards. It was the end of a promising judicial career.

REQUESTS TO INTERVENE

In the meantime, my staff had been reporting to me what they were hearing outside our courtroom. They said that some lawyers were very happy to learn that their cases were raffled to me, while others were afraid to the point that they would withdraw their case, only to re-file it later in order that it would be raffled or assigned to another judge. They opined that the first group of lawyers were those with meritorious cases, while the other group were those with weak or losing cases and were hoping to pull strings or do some "fixing" in order to win. It was commonly known in Quezon City who are the judges who could be "fixed" and those who could not.

Probably because of my reputation, some people with cases before other branches would ask my help, through my staff, about their cases. The problem is, I did not want to interfere with cases pending before other judges, in the same manner that I did not want them to be calling me for any case. This is because on my part, I am sure that I will study each case very thoroughly. Thus, meritorious cases are sure to win, and those without merit will surely lose, depending on the evidence presented. No amount of intervention would sway my judgment.

Sometimes, winning respondents in other branches come to us for help in getting copies of judgments after their cases had been dismissed by order in open court. For some unexplained reasons, copies of the resolutions are not released to their lawyers for long periods, necessitating their queries.

It is in such instances that we help the parties get copies of the resolution or order of dismissal in their favor.

Some people come to us to denounce certain judges who were asking for "something" in consideration of their cases. In such cases, I tell the party that I cannot interfere, but I advised them to file administrative cases in the Supreme Court against the judge concerned. If they agreed and wanted my help, I usually called a stenographer to dictate their story in the form of a complaint-affidavit based on the stories they related. I let them read the affidavit while still in draft form. The party concerned always looked satisfied, and would tell me that they will sign it, and eventually file it. In the meantime, while it is being finalized, they usually excused themselves to get something to eat or do something else outside. But in all such instances, the parties concerned never came back to sign or get the affidavit. Obviously, they are afraid to file cases against judges.

ENCOUNTERS WITH LOCAL GOVERNMENT OFFICIALS

One day, I received a telephone call from a staff of the Mayor of Quezon City, saying that the Mayor was very much interested in a certain case. He gave me the docket number as well as the parties for which the Mayor was interceding. When I looked into the case, I found that there were two opposing groups both with the surname of the Mayor who were locked in a property dispute. After studying the case, I concluded that I could not make a ruling favorable to the group mentioned. I prayed so hard about it, before and after I finalized the decision.

The reason for my apprehension was because the judges of Quezon City were being given a special monthly allowance by the city government, just as other cities are doing to their judges with authority from the Supreme Court, albeit in varying amounts. Earlier, I had heard that the Mayor of Caloocan City cancelled the allowance of all their judges after one judge denied his request for a favorable decision in a certain case.

So, fearful that our Mayor would feel aggrieved by my decision and decide to retaliate by canceling the judges' allowance, I prayed that he would withhold only my allowance and let the others continue enjoying theirs.

A few weeks after the promulgation of my decision on the case, the Quezon City judges had a luncheon to which the City Mayor was invited. When the Mayor arrived, I greeted him with trepidation. After he shook hands with all the judges one by one, I sat on a distant seat, farthest from where he was. To my horror, he walked all the way and opted to sit beside me. I was really afraid that he would berate me for my decision, and/or announce the end of our allowances. I could hardly taste the food served to us.

When I found the courage to speak, I told the Mayor how sorry I was that I could not find any reason to decide in favor of his group. He seemed not to understand what I was saying. When I explained what the case was about, he appeared enlightened and said that that case involved some of his half brothers and sisters and other relatives, and that I should decide it as I know best. I was so relieved, especially on behalf of my colleagues, who need not lose their special allowances because of me.

It was then that I realized that the Mayor did not authorize the caller to call me about the case.

A similar thing happened in the case of the then Vice Mayor of Quezon City, who was my co-member in the Board of Trustees of the Quezon City Youth Development Foundation (QCYDF), a non-government organization which was working for the benefit of underprivileged youth.

I once received a handwritten note on the memo pad of the Vice Mayor, asking my help in another case. I do not remember the particulars of the case, but I do remember that I could not, and did not, decide in favor of the person named in his note. When I saw him at our next meeting of the QCYDF,

I tried to explain to him the reasons for deciding the way I did. As in the case of the Mayor, he knew nothing about the note, and told me to forget it. It must have been foisted on him by someone from his office.

These instances made me steadfast in my desire to continue deciding cases according to the evidence presented before me, and not due to any pressure or *"pakiusap."* It was a tougher path to follow, but thankfully, God has always delivered me through.

To Gain Or Not To Gain

ON SHERIFFS AND GIFTS

In my time as a trial judge, the sheriffs in most courts were considered the most corrupt. This is because they are the ones who execute or implement the judgments of the courts, and in so doing, they can demand a fee before actually doing their work. Winning parties and their lawyers are often willing to come across to see the fruition of their victories, otherwise they might be waiting forever.

Sheriffs are also the most approachable among the court staff, because their work usually takes them outside the office. Thus, they could become fixers for unscrupulous parties. It is not surprising therefore that sheriffs could buy cars, don signature-brand shirts, send their children to exclusive schools, and celebrate their birthdays or Christmas parties with ostentatious display of wealth.

But not my court Sheriff. I carefully selected him from members of my own church, after checking his integrity and moral fitness before I recommended him to the Supreme Court for appointment.

My Sheriff once informed me that he was approached by a prominent lawyer, asking how much his judge is worth, but he answered: *"Forget it, Sir, she is not for sale."*

One time, a lawyer reported during a hearing that he spent so much for the execution of a judgment in favor of his client. I called for my Sheriff and asked him in open court how much he received from the lawyer and how he spent it. He reported that he got ₱3,000 and paid for truck rental, three laborers, and two policemen who accompanied them to keep order during the execution. After he gave an itemized report with the total amount spent, I told him to return the balance of about P100. The lawyer was saying: *"No more, Your Honor. It's okay, Your Honor."* But I insisted. In a short while, the news spread out that I was the only judge who was asking his/her Sheriff to account in open court for his expenses in executing judgments.

It is through the sheriffs that lawyers and litigants learn of the birthdays of the judge or when a particular branch would be celebrating its Christmas party. In my case, I silently celebrate my birthdays with my staff. We keep the date of our intended Christmas celebrations to ourselves.

However, during one of our Christmas parties, there were two *lechons* that unexpectedly came from a litigant. When told about it, I asked my staff not to accept them, and so they politely told the two couriers to return them to the giver, despite the pleas of the two couriers to let them leave the *lechons* with us for the reason that it will be very cumbersome for them to carry them back to whoever sent them.

Sometime later, we learned that the couriers gave them instead to the sheriffs who were having their own party at the same time as ours. And the sheriffs gladly accepted them! I wonder if the sender ever learned that we did not accept his *lechons*.

The same thing happened when a box with a signature-brand cake was being delivered to us from a litigant whose case was already decided. The delivery boy explained that the cake was only a token of appreciation for our fast and favorable ruling. His pleas for us to accept the cake fell on deaf ears. He left, but we do not know if he properly returned it to the sender.

There were many other gifts that we similarly rejected, but I never learned what were inside if they were gift-wrapped. The only gifts I allowed my staff to receive were corporate giveaways for Christmas, like calendars or other similar items, which are given to all and not to a particular judge in consideration of any case. Of course, friends without cases who course their Christmas presents through the court for convenience are also exempted from this general rule.

THE OFFERS GET BIGGER

In June of 1988, some areas of the Quezon City Hall which were used as offices were gutted by fire. Among the offices that were burned down were several branches of the RTC and MeTC, including my own, as well as the Office of the Register of Deeds. Case records and land titles that were reduced to ashes had to be reconstituted judicially. I handled quite a number of such cases.

Some people took advantage of this by filing petitions for reconstitution of land titles of certain pieces of land over which they had dubious titles. One particular case caught my attention. It was a petition for reconstitution of a large tract of land in Diliman, Quezon City. Mr. Q, the petitioner, presented a photocopy of a very old title which was so blurred and almost illegible. He testified that he acquired the subject land by purchase, although he could no longer present a copy of the Deed of Sale which was registered many years ago.

When I examined the evidence, I computed the age of the petitioner which he gave at the time of his testimony as against the date of issuance of the title, and found that he would have been only six years old on the date of his alleged acquisition. For lack of any convincing evidence that he had the means (at the age of 6!) to buy the big tract and that he really owned it, I was poised to deny the petition.

Before I could draft my ruling, I got a visit from Judge T, a fellow RTC Judge in Quezon City. He showed me two duly signed and notarized Deeds of Sale in my favor over two prime lots in Quezon City. When I asked what it was all about, he said that I was being given the two lots in consideration of my favorable ruling on the petition of Mr. Q. I almost fell from my chair. After gaining my composure, I found myself giving a "sermon" to Judge T, who was much younger than I and several years my junior in the judiciary. I told him that he still had a long way to go, and a bright future was before him. He could still reach the top of the judicial ladder if he performs well. Doing well means not only acting with competence and efficiency, but also with unquestionable integrity. I told him that he should never allow himself to enter into any transaction to favor any judge in exchange for a favorable ruling in any case, and that a case should be decided only upon its merits and not in consideration of any extraneous matter.

I then informed Judge T that I had already studied the case and found the petition without merit; that I will be dismissing the case; and that I will not change my mind because of the gift of the two lots, which I will not accept anyway. Judge T was obviously embarrassed. He tore the documents into pieces in my presence, said "sorry" and left.

Wonder of all wonders, Judge T was also promoted to the Court of Appeals several years after me. I found out that he had a very powerful politician for a backer. I just hope that he did not enter into any questionable transactions after my "sermon."

THE BIGGEST OFFER

Cases involving violation of the Bouncing Checks Law (Batas Pambansa [BP] 22) have been clogging the dockets of the courts since its enactment. Somehow, the courts have become "collecting agencies" because the usual purpose of complainants who file criminal cases against the issuer of unfunded checks is to collect, and not necessarily to put the issuer/drawer of the check behind bars.

Each check that bounces constitutes one case; hence, there could be as many cases as there are bouncing checks. It is possible that many such cases between the same parties are raffled to different branches of the court. Thus, for convenience, the parties may file a motion to have these cases consolidated and assigned to one particular branch. Once the complainant is paid the value of the subject check, he usually loses interest to pursue the criminal case.

The biggest amount I have ever handled in a BP 22 case involved the sale of several parcels of land amounting to millions of pesos, where the buyer paid by issuing fifteen checks that bounced and became the subject of fifteen BP 22 cases. Six of such cases landed in my RTC branch, while the rest were assigned to another judge. In the course of the trial, we noted a technical defect in the Information, for which the defense counsel filed a consolidated Motion to Dismiss the six cases.

As I was studying the motion and after doing some research on the matter, I found that no jurisprudence has been issued by the Supreme Court on that particular issue. I then resolved to make further research to guide me in resolving the motion.

The records of the six cases were on top of my desk when I got a visit from Judge D, the judge assigned to the nine companion cases, and who had just retired the week before. He was asking me to dismiss the six cases before me, as he had already done with the nine assigned to him. Pointing to the records on my desk, I answered that I was in fact making a thorough study and research on the novel issue involved.

"I-dismiss mo na," he said. *"May 3M diyan,"* he further stated while making a sign of "3" with his last three fingers and a circular sign with his thumb and forefinger.

"What do you mean?" I asked incredulously.

"Yes, there's three million pesos there for the dismissal of those cases."

My eyes became misty as they usually do when I am mad, but I held back my tears. I felt both insulted and angry that he would make such an offer to me. If he were not only much older than me, I could have punched him and ordered him out of my room posthaste. When I was able to collect myself, I told him that I have not and will never collect any single centavo for any case, and that he should leave me alone so that I could study the issues very well.

"Baka lang sakali," he said and left.

I sat still for a while, trying to compose myself. Judge D was obviously having difficulty in walking as he had to be assisted by somebody when he walked, probably because of his extra large body frame or due to some kind of illness. And yet he had the temerity to walk to my office to offer P3M for dismissing those cases. No wonder he had a very ostentatious and lavish dinner during his retirement! I wondered how much he would earn by interceding for these cases before me.

Just then, Atty. Glo, my Branch Clerk of Court (BCC) came rushing to my chambers.

"*Judge,*" she exclaimed. "*Judge D called me to go out with him after coming from here. He told me that he had already talked to you about the dismissal of the cases on your desk. He asked me to draft the order of dismissal and he will take care of me ('Ako na ang bahala sa yo'). He gave this for me to copy.*" She showed me a piece of paper, which turned out to be Judge D's order of dismissal of the nine related BP 22 cases assigned to him.

I was livid. I told my BCC that until then, I was still weighing the options because of the novel legal issue involved in the cases. But because of the ₱3M offer, I will not anymore study how to dismiss the cases; instead, I will concentrate on reasoning out why the cases should not be dismissed. I knew that if I did dismiss the cases, Judge D would be richer by millions of pesos at the expense of my name.

After issuing my resolution denying the motion to dismiss, it was challenged by *certiorari* before the Court of Appeals. I then told my family that I would probably be reversed by a higher court for the first time in my life. But the appellate court, instead of reversing my order, affirmed it with praises for the judicious way I resolved the novel issue involved.

Some people who later heard of Judge D's offer said that I was crazy to reject it. Back then, our salary was a paltry ₱13,000 per month, such that if I already retired, I would not receive even half of ₱3M as retirement gratuity. Had I accepted, I could have gone around the world, built or procured a mansion as my residence, enjoyed life and still have had funds for rainy days. But as for me, I have no regrets. I was not ashamed of the humble one-storey home we lived in at that time or the simple lifestyle I led. Besides, I was reminded of this Biblical verse: "*For what will it profit a man if he gains the whole world and forfeits his life?*" (*Matthew 16:26*) Indeed, no amount of riches would ever be sufficient in exchange for a clear conscience and one's peace of mind.

ॐ ॐ

Experiences at the Court of Appeals

The work in the Court of Appeals (CA) is quite different from that in the trial court. In the latter court, the judge is the sole and single authority, while in the CA, we always acted in a division of three justices each, the most senior of which is the Chairman, the next in seniority according to the hierarchy of the court is the senior member, and the latest appointee is the junior member. The one assigned to study the case and to draft the ruling is called the *ponente*.

No judgment or resolution can ever be promulgated without the concurrence and signatures of all three members of the division. When they cannot agree or when there is a dissent, two more justices are selected by raffle to make a special division of five members. The special division of five should deliberate, and shall decide upon the concurrence of at least three out of the five members.

In routine matters, like in actions on motions for extension of time to file pleadings, the *ponente* just drafts the resolution and passes such action to the other members for their signature. But in litigious matters, there should be a deliberation among the division members. In my case, when I became a division chairman, I set a particular day for our weekly deliberations.

Whenever there is a permanent vacancy in the position of the Division Chairman through promotion, resignation, permanent disability or death, there is a reorganization of the divisions. This is how a member is transferred from one division to another until he reaches the top.

During my time in the CA, appealed cases were raffled twice (though not anymore now). The first raffle is made to assign a *ponente* who shall take charge of drafting resolutions during what we call "completion stage", *i.e.*, where the resolutions are only for purposes of directing the parties to file their appellant's brief, appellee's brief, reply brief and other routine matters. When all the requisite pleadings shall have been submitted, a resolution is issued declaring the case submitted for decision; after which, the record is returned to the Raffle Division for re-raffling to another *ponente* to study the case and draft the decision.

In cases of re-organizations, I always prayed that I will be teamed with members who are honest and upright, so that I would be spared from being teamed with anyone who succumbs to temptations of under-the-table deals, which I heard was happening in some cases.

IN THE NAME OF A JUSTICE

One day, a member of my division came to me and said that a friend of his had complained that a justice in an appealed case in the CA was asking for P20,000 for a favorable decision. He checked the case number and found that it was assigned to me. Of course he did not believe that I could do such a thing, as he said he knew my reputation, and that is why he came to see me about it. I thus lost no time in asking my staff to produce the record of the mentioned case.

Together, we found that the case was assigned to me while it was still in the completion stage. Why should a justice who is just the "completion justice" ask for P20,000 when that person will not be the one to decide the case? My colleague thus concluded that it was just the lawyer who was using the name of a justice to extort money from his client. He then advised his friend to change his lawyer.

THE JAUNDICED LAWYER

In the CA, we lady justices customarily gave *"pasalubong"* to our lady colleagues after coming from abroad. On a particular day, after emerging from a hearing on an application for injunction, I was handed by my daughter Grace, who was then my Chief of Staff, a small gift-wrapped box which, she said, was given by Justice S for me. Since I knew that she (Justice S) had been abroad, I surmised that it was a *pasalubong*. When I opened it, the name of the lawyer-giver was inside, and so was a set of diamond earrings, ring and necklace. The lawyer-giver had just filed a Motion for Reconsideration (MR) of a decision I had promulgated against her client.

I felt my blood rising to my head. Justice S had been asking me in the past to rule favorably on some cases she was interceding for. Among her tactics was to say, *"Ibigay mo na to pa-birthday sa akin"* or *"Pagbigyan mo naman ako, Darling."* I remember that I had recused myself from further handling the cases when I knew that I could not give in to her requests. So, she is still at it!!! When will Justice S stop from interceding in losing cases?

On the other hand the lawyer-giver (Atty. QL) used to be an associate justice of the CA, but was purged during a judiciary reorganization, and is now in the private practice of law. Some of my colleagues describe her as "jaundiced" because she always glitters in gold as she wears lots of golden diamond-clad jewelry on her body. Now, she is gifting me with an expensive set of jewelry for obvious reasons: she wanted a favorable action on her MR pending before me.

I then ran to the chambers of Justice S to return the jewelry. With trembling hands, I said, *"I feel very insulted with this gift. You and QL must have noticed that I wear only custom or fancy jewelry. But I am proud to wear only what I can afford. I do not need this, and I will not wear this type of jewelry, especially in consideration of any case. And please stop interfering in any of my cases."*

Justice S tried to embrace and hug me, saying, *"No more na, Darling,"* but I brushed her aside and hurriedly left the room. It was a good thing that Justice S had a visitor , a private practitioner, who witnessed the return, lest she make the giver believe that I accepted her gift.

HALF A MILLION FOR ACQUITTAL?

In a case of robbery that was assigned to me, a lawyer in my staff whom I assigned to research on it submitted her report with the recommendation that the crime be downgraded, and that the accused be convicted only for theft, in the absence of proof that the accused used force upon things or intimidation of persons — two important elements of the offense of robbery — in allegedly taking the subject property consisting of a few pieces of rusty galvanized iron sheets.

When I reviewed her report, I found that one important element of theft was missing, *i.e.,* intent to gain. How could the accused take away some galvanized iron sheets when the Mayor had posted guards on the construction site? Moreover, the filing of the case appeared to be more of political vendetta against a city counselor who belonged to the opposite party of the Mayor. So in my *ponencia,* I decided to acquit the accused, a certain Counselor CC. The other members of my division concurred in my decision.

A few weeks after the promulgation of our judgment of acquittal, Atty. B, one of the division clerks of court of the CA, informed us that CC is her former classmate; that when the latter came to get a copy of our judgment, he (CC) informed her that he was happy for having been vindicated through his acquittal although he became poorer by half a million pesos. When she asked who was the *ponente,* he answered, "Justice

Magtolis." She retorted that she could not believe it because she knows the reputation of Justice Magtolis as 'clean'. But he said he parted with ₱500,000 anyway.

Curious, Atty. B asked CC, *"To whom did you deliver the money? Direct ba kay Justice Magtolis?"* He answered, *"Of course not. My lawyer delivered it."* Atty B. thus informed my researcher about her conversation with CC.

Naturally, I asked for the case records. I found out that the defense counsel was Atty. DC, the estranged husband of one of our lady colleagues in the Court, who was notorious for winning his cases by using the name of his wife. I'm sure that he never came to see me about the case. But just then, it flashed in my mind that a male colleague had called me about it, but as usual, I forgot the case number and the name of the accused. As in all other cases, I considered nothing but the evidence in writing the decision.

I lost no time in calling the wife, Justice DC, expressing my anger and disgust at her husband for using my name to extort a large amount from his client. She in turn called her husband, echoing my anger. A few days later, I received a letter from Atty. DC, expressing regrets and apology for his unintentional besmirching of my name and reputation which he allegedly knew to be unsullied. He explained that the amount he asked CC was not for me but for his legal researcher.

The reason given was very incredible. Lawyers who employ researchers pay them regular salaries, not a per-case fee. In any case, no lawyer in his right mind will pay such a substantial sum to his own legal researcher for just one case.

Be that as it may, I was glad that at least I had a concrete document to show that no portion of the ₱500,000 went to me. I just asked that the letter be photocopied, and a copy sent to CC.

A SCHOLARSHIP FOR GRACE

A letter coming from someone with a Chinese-sounding name and addressed to my daughter Grace was received in my office at the CA one day. It offered full scholarship for her who was then in her first year of her law studies in the Ateneo de Manila University.

Naturally, Grace showed me the letter and I got curious as to who would make such an offer. I thus asked my staff to check our index of cases to find out if the writer has a pending case before me. It turned out that he had a case which I decided against him when I was still a trial judge, and that that decision was then on appeal before the CA. We just ignored the letter and it went straight to the wastebasket.

One day, the writer of the letter went to our office and verbally repeated his offer to Grace. I was in my chambers at that time and so I did not see this person. My daughter politely declined the offer and said she was able to afford paying for her tuition fee in law school through her salary from the CA. The man was insistent and said he would even pay for her books if she would research on his case. Grace firmly said that she would not accept it, after which, the man left. It was a strange offer, but apparently, people would attempt to do anything to gain what they wanted.

A PROCESS SERVER FALLS

In the Court of Appeals, our resolutions are promulgated through the Office of the Division Clerk of Court (DCC). Each division has a DCC. We also have Process Servers who deliver/serve our judgments, resolutions, orders and other court processes within the National Capital Region (NCR) to the lawyers and litigants concerned. Our DCC in my last years in office was Atty. Madarang.

Among the cases assigned to me was the appeal of ML who was convicted of homicide instead of murder by the RTC of Pasig City, and was incarcerated in the New Bilibid Prison (NBP) in Muntinlupa City. During the pendency of the appeal, ML through counsel filed an application for bail. Because homicide is a bailable offense and in view of the Constitutional right of the accused to bail, we approved the application for bail and directed the issuance of an order of release in favor of the accused after he posts the required bond and its approval by our division.

Before Atty. Madarang could prepare the order of release, Process Server CS came to her to hurry up the order of release. It was almost the close of office hours, so CS assisted in the mechanical process of collating the requisite documents and stapling them together. He then got all the papers, saying he would deliver them to the NBP first hour on the following day. As is usual for process servers, CS also brought with him three or four other documents for service to other people on the same day.

At about two o'clock the following day, Atty. Madarang got a phone call from a certain Lyn who introduced herself as a relative of ML, and asked her how much more they have to pay for the latter's release. She told Atty. Madarang that they have coordinated with RV, a clerk in the RTC of Pasig City (from where the case originated), and wanted to know whether the amount quoted by RV to be paid to Justice Magtolis was correct.

Atty. Madarang lost no time in reporting this to me. Together, we devised a plot to find out the truth about the "arrangement" for ML's release. She called the RTC of Pasig and asked for RV, introducing herself to be Alice, a relative of ML. RV happened to be out then, but a certain Bing answered her call, saying, *"Wala si RV, pero kahapon pa niya kayong inaantay. Meron pa kasi kayong babayaran. Ipapa-en banc pa kasi yon ni Justice Magtolis."* (RV is out but she has been waiting for you since yesterday because you still have to pay something. Justice Magtolis has still to submit the case to the Court *en banc*.)

[*N.B.*- This is obviously a ploy for extortion. At that point in time, no further action was needed from the Court as we had already issued a resolution for the accused's release. Besides, it is contrary to procedures, because the Court *en banc* never acts on cases, only on ceremonial or business matters pertaining to the administration of the Court.]

After getting the mobile phone number of CS, Atty. Madarang, pretending to be RV, began texting him. Through an exchange of text messages with CS, Atty. Madarang found out that CS has been waiting for a certain Art, a relative of accused ML. It turned out that CS did not immediately deliver the Order of Release to the Director of Prisons and the Defense Counsel who was waiting there, as he should have done.

Finally, at about 4:00 P.M. CS texted the caller-relative (who was really Atty. Madarang in disguise) that he had met with Art, and that ML was already with him.

We found out that CS was not able to serve (deliver) the other court processes he brought with him, because he spent almost the whole day in the NBP until the arrival of Art and the release of ML.

When Atty. Madarang confronted CS the following day, he broke down and asked for forgiveness, saying that he won't do it again. The same thing happened when she brought him to my office. He asked that if ever I will file a case against him, he begged me to let the holidays pass so that he will still receive the year-end benefits usually given to court employees, at least for the sake of his children.

I was torn between justice and mercy. Should I just let the incident pass for the sake of his children? Or should I charge him administratively, so that he and others like him who use their office to extort money from litigants will learn a lesson?

Of course I had a problem because we had no direct proof that money passed in the case of ML's release. Still, I was convinced that he did something wrong, since he neglected his duties by not delivering the papers promptly to the Director of Prisons, by not personally delivering the copy for the defense counsel but to the accused's relative, and by failing to serve the other documents he was supposed to serve during the day.

As to his plea for mercy, I knew he would not be prejudiced by a disciplinary action because it was only October then, and the requirements of due process will surely stand on the way of an early resolution, such that he will surely receive the legislated 13th month pay and other bonuses given during Christmastime.

I filed an administrative case against CS for neglect of duty and misconduct in office. Atty. Madarang was my main witness. A surprise witness was an inmate of the Correctional Institute for Women who informed me that CS had approached her, offering to work for her release in consideration of ₱20,000. However, she did not have the amount; hence, she remained incarcerated. She mentioned a former co-inmate who got the same offer from CS, was able to raise the amount, and thereafter gained her freedom. Unfortunately, we could no longer locate the latter.

This notwithstanding, the Investigating Official, CA Assistant Clerk of Court Elisa Longalong, found CS guilty as charged and recommended that he be suspended for one-and-a-half years. Since it is the Supreme Court which has disciplinary authority over judges and court personnel, her recommendation was forwarded to the High Court. The same was affirmed by the Supreme Court in its decision which became a landmark or precedent-setting jurisprudence insofar as the admissibility of electronic evidence (text messages) is concerned.

☙ ❧

The Case of the TRO

In the early months of the year 2000, the mass media had a heyday reporting on the apparent manipulation of the shares of stocks of the BW Corporation (BWC) that made instant billionaires of certain people and paupers out of others. It was alleged that high-ranking officials of the land had a hand when the shares of stocks of BWC were bought in bulk by the group of XXX at a giveaway price, but the stocks had a sudden increment in value, such that the latter were able to sell them at tremendous profit to the group of AAA before the stocks suddenly fell again, resulting in heavy losses to AAA and company.

Because of the high profile and sensationalism that attended the transactions, the Department of Justice (DOJ) and the Securities and Exchange Commission (SEC) were constrained to conduct investigations of the transactions.

While the investigations were in progress, a case for prohibition and injunction with prayer for a temporary restraining order (TRO) was filed with the Court of Appeals, praying that the DOJ and SEC be stopped/restrained from proceeding on their investigations. The case was raffled to Justice B, the senior member of the division which I chaired at that time.

Justice B immediately prepared the draft of a resolution granting a TRO. When it was passed on to me, and after reading the petition, I formed the opinion that a TRO was not in order. Nevertheless, I called for a conference/ deliberation of our division where Justice B strongly

45

defended his position that a TRO should issue. When we could not agree, I set the application for TRO for immediate hearing; after which, we deliberated again, but our respective positions remained unchanged. Justice D, our Junior member agreed with me. But still, we had no unanimity.

I then borrowed the records of the case to bring home and make a closer and more thorough study of the issues involved. As a result of my study, I became more convinced that a TRO was not proper. Thus, I wrote a Memorandum to Justice B, enumerating five (5) reasons why we should not issue a TRO, and informing him that if he still disagreed with me, I will be forced to write a dissenting opinion in which case, a division of five will be created pursuant to our Internal Rules to decide the issue.

The following day, I received an unexpected visit from a long-lost friend who, after the usual amenities, told me that I was the only one who had not signed the TRO in the BWC case, and requesting that I too sign the same so that it could be promulgated immediately. This came as a surprise. How come there are two signatories when I knew for a fact that the Junior member concurred with my opinion? And how did this guy know that I was the only one who had not signed?

These are intriguing questions that remained unsaid, since CA judgments, resolutions and orders are not supposed to be divulged to anyone outside the Division concerned until they are properly promulgated. In the course of our conversation, I learned that a high government official had sent him to me. I politely told him that I will check and study the records some more, and we shall soon issue a resolution.

I lost no time in calling Justice D, to ask her why she signed when she told me earlier that she agreed with me. The latter explained that she was forced to sign upon the persuasion of Justice B. She felt that being a Junior member, she could not shun nor overcome the prodding of a more senior member. I told her, she should be ready for the consequences because the case involves public interest, and she signed against her better judgment. She was a bit alarmed, and so she told me that she will also borrow the records like I did, and state her final position afterwards.

The following day, Justice D came to my office to show that she had erased her signature using correction fluid on the resolution prepared by Justice B, and she had written above it, "I agree with the Memorandum dated such-and-such of Justice Magtolis."

Early the following morning, while still at home, I got calls from several friends outside the Court, commending me for my courageous stand. My children also got phone calls saying, "I'm glad that your mom is there." The callers learned from the headline news of the Philippines Daily Inquirer (PDI), one of the most widely-circulated newspapers in the country, that the Court of Appeals had issued a TRO signed only by Justice B, and that I as Chairperson and Justice D as the third member of the division, had no signature on it. Through the newspaper on the way to the office, I also learned that Justice B had indeed promulgated his resolution granting a TRO with his lone signature on it.

I went directly to the Office of Atty. Madarang, our Division Clerk of Court (DCC) to ask why she released the resolution with only one signature, although I and Justice D were just in our respective offices the day before when it was promulgated. The DCC explained that when Justice B came to her office asking her to immediately promulgate the resolution with only his signature, she wanted to run up to my office to get my advice /instruction, but Justice B scolded her, telling her to just follow his instructions. She showed me a handwritten note signed by Justice B, saying that he was ordering its release on the strength of a Rules of Court provision that a lone justice may issue a TRO. She knew that the rule cited allows a single justice to issue a TRO only in case of extreme urgency when the two other members of the division are absent, none of which circumstances were present in this case. But how could she disobey the orders of a justice?

When I proceeded to my office, I found it like a marketplace with so many people at my door. After passing incognito through the crowd, I learned that they were people from the mass media, wanting to interview me about the case. I instructed my staff to announce that I would not be giving interviews, but they could check the records from our DCC. The next day, my memorandum was quoted in full in the next issue of the PDI. Follow up news were carried on its front page in the following days.

Some columnists in various newspapers gave their personal opinions about it. One columnist even opined, "There must be a million and one reasons why a single justice issued a TRO." Telephone calls followed later, inviting me to appear at some talk shows. But again, I declined all such invitations, in order that no one will ever think that my action/inaction was made to seek publicity.

The Supreme Court directed the CA Presiding Justice to investigate and report about it. The CA Presiding Justice did an investigation, but no administrative case was pursued against anyone. Instead, the SC issued, in a subsequent judgment involving a question on TRO, definitive rules on when and how a single justice may issue a TRO: (a) in cases of emergency, (b) when the two other members of the division are out or absent, in which case the two other members should state their positions on the following working day, on whether they agreed or disagreed with the resolution.

When Justice B followed up his TRO with a resolution granting an injunction, I wrote a dissenting opinion, but he did not report my dissent to the Presiding Justice so that a special division of five members could be created to tackle the issues on the BWC case.

He also sat for a long time on the Motion for Reconsideration filed by the respondents. Although I sent him a memo to remind him to act on it within the reglementary period, he never replied to my memo nor acted on the motion. I surmise that he was waiting for a reorganization of the Court which would result in our being assigned to different divisions.

When such reorganization took place, and pursuant to our Internal Rules, we were separated, and he carried the case to his new division. I never tried to find out how he decided the case on the merits, lest I appear to be personally interested on the case.

೪ ૭

Justice With Mercy

DOOR JAMBS

A poor and struggling maker of wooden doors and jambs from Taytay, Rizal filed a case for collection of sum of money against a wealthy couple who ordered doors and jambs for renovation of their mansion in Quezon City, but refused to pay. The poor contractor was represented by a provincial lawyer, while the couple had a battery of seasoned lawyers. The latter took advantage of the fact that the poor contractor had no printed delivery receipts and was using only notebook pages as proof of delivery. The defendants' counsels tried to discredit such papers, setting forth the defense that the ordered materials were never delivered. They used an intimidating voice when cross-examining the plaintiff-contractor who alone testified for himself.

The plaintiff stood his ground, describing how he was personally contracted by the defendant-husband, the dates and time of his delivery, the sizes of the doors and jambs, the description/design of the doors and what portion of the house they were for. He also identified the defendant-wife who usually received the orders and signed the delivery receipts.

No amount of oratory before the court, nor the intimidating tone and menacing looks at the poor plaintiff from the defendants' counsels could crush the plaintiff's testimony, who obviously could not afford a good lawyer. The court rendered justice in favor of the plaintiff.

INCESTUOUS RAPE

A 13-year old girl was raped by her father several times while her mom was in the province to breathe sea air in the hope that her tuberculosis could be healed. As the father seemed to have no qualms about repeatedly doing it, she confided to her teacher, who alerted some sisters in a religious institution. The latter took the girl into their custody and reported the incestuous rape to the police, which instituted two criminal cases of rape against the father. Only two cases were filed because the girl could only remember the dates of the first and last time of occurrence.

During the pre-trial conference, the father vehemently denied having touched his daughter. He branded the "false" report as her retaliation to his having scolded her for going out too much with boys. He insisted on his innocence. Nothing positive came out during the pre-trial conference, and even plea bargaining failed; hence, the case proceeded to trial immediately.

At the trial, the prosecutor called the girl-complainant to be its first witness. When she was asked to state her name and other personal circumstances, she stammered with her first name, but could not pronounce her surname, indicating that she was so traumatized and could not accept the fact that she belonged to her father's family. Instead, she cried copiously, such that I had to suspend trial, ordered a glass of water to be served her, and called for another pre-trial conference.

I explained to both the accused and his counsel as well as to the prosecutor that forcing the girl to testify and recall her ordeal would probably cause more damage emotionally and psychologically, so I suggested that they reconsider plea bargaining.

The defense offered to have the accused plead guilty to acts of lasciviousness. However, the applicable penalty for such an offense is not more than six months. I considered it too light, fearful that once he regains his freedom, the accused might rape again not only the complainant but her two younger sisters living with them as well. I suggested two counts of qualified seduction in which case, the imprisonment ranges from eight years and one day to twelve years. After serving the penalties for the two cases, the father would be much older and would probably not molest any daughter anymore. Surprisingly, the accused agreed to plead guilty to the latter offense. So, the trial was terminated, and I pronounced the sentence right away. The nuns who accompanied the complainant as well as the doctor who was supposed to testify were all praises for the way I handled the case which ended without the girl's having to recall her traumatic ordeal.

ILLEGAL ADOPTION

As a family court judge, I rendered lots of cases granting adoption of children by well-meaning would-be adopters. The adopting parents were always appreciative of the expeditious way we handled the cases with positive results. But there was a case which was opposed by the State through the Office of the Solicitor General (OSG).

The case was filed by a Filipina wife and her American husband, intending to adopt a 10-year old girl who grew up with the petitioner-wife after having been abandoned as a baby by her parents who were insurgents. The spouses wanted to bring the girl with them to the United States, and so they filed a joint petition.

At the conclusion of the trial, the Solicitor filed a strong opposition on the ground that the petitioner-husband was not qualified. Although he possessed all other qualifications, his age of 25 years disqualifies him because of the required 16-year age difference between an adopter and the adopted. On the other hand, the wife, though fully qualified, cannot adopt singly because the law requires that married couples must jointly adopt.

In deciding the case, I wrestled with the following questions: What will happen to the girl if I denied the petition? As she had known no other parent except the petitioner-wife, and lately, also the petitioner-husband, how will she fend for herself if the spouses left for the USA without her? Can she find her dissident parents in the mountains? What kind of life will she have with parents who are always moving and hiding or at war with law enforcers? What will her future be, since no other relative came out to volunteer to take care of her? The Social Worker who conducted the case study likewise did not find any of her relatives.

I decided the case on the principle that in all cases concerning children, his/her best interests and welfare should be the primary consideration. I granted the petition despite the legal constraints. The OSG appealed to the Court of Appeals (CA). The appellate Court justice who reviewed the case affirmed my decision with praises saying, *"...the good judge breathed life into the law"*.

THE MOTHER, THE CULPRIT

A rather unique case started with a report made by employees of a government office. Their attention was attracted by the frequent crying of a boy who they used to see with a woman-beggar who was apparently his mother, lying or sitting on cardboard boxes spread out at a corner near the Office of the Government Corporate Counsel (OGCC). They found out that he was crying whenever the mother would suck his genitals. Alarmed, they called the Department of Social Welfare and Development (DSWD), which sent social workers to the place. Finding and observing the report to be true, the social workers took both mother and son to their office for temporary shelter.

The law against child abuse was not yet enacted then. The DSWD thus filed only a petition for involuntary deprivation of parental custody and authority against the mother (let's call her Madder), which landed in my sala. I ordered Madder to be separated from her son (Biboy) . The latter was housed in a boy's reception center for children, and the mother in a home for unwed mothers.

I appointed two separate sets of professionals to attend to them, *i.e.* social workers, psychologists and psychiatrists to conduct case studies and medical, psychological and psychiatric examinations/evaluations of both mother and child. The Social Worker for Biboy was to act as his temporary guardian (*guardian ad litem*), aside from conducting the case studies.

On the first date of hearing, the Social Worker arrived ahead with Biboy. When Madder entered the courtroom, the handsome Biboy automatically put his knees together tightly, and would not even look at his mother.

From the reports of the social workers, psychologists and psychiatrists, the Court learned that Biboy was about two years old, the second son of Madder. The elder son is already in the custody of Madder's father (the maternal grandfather) who refused to take custody of Madder and Biboy for the reason that he can no longer afford any additional mouths to feed.

The medical and psychiatric reports indicated that Madder is suffering from a serious case of schizophrenia and will not be able to hold any regular job. On the other hand, Biboy appeared to be rather thin. What is worse, his genitalia was bluish and swollen. Madder does not want to live anywhere else except at the street corner where they were found begging because it is there where her Japanese "husband" would come back for her.

Biboy has no Japanese features and is apparently sired by a Caucasian father as shown by his physical appearance. Because Madder had expressed that she would fight to death to have her son returned to her at all costs, I asked Biboy to approach his mother, but he stood rigid, holding on to the social worker, and did not come any inch closer to his mother.

After hearing both sets of witnesses, I decided that it would be to the best interest of Biboy if he is separated from his mother, who apparently has no means to raise her son properly, as her recovery from her illness was described as remote. Moreover, her companionship, aside from living on the street, is wreaking havoc on the boy's normal psychological, emotional and even physical development.

Thus, despite the legal provision that no child below seven years of age shall be separated from the mother, I declared that there were special circumstances justifying a deviation from such regular or general rule. I decided to remove custody and parental authority of Madder over her 2-year old son, placed him in an institution under the supervision of the DSWD and declared him available for legal adoption. As for Madder, she was to be under medical supervision while continuing to be housed in the institution for unwed mothers.

⚛⚛

More Lessons from the Bench

EARLY JITTERS

The work of a judge is two-fold: adjudicatory and administrative. Adjudicatory work is further divided into two categories: (a) conducting hearings or trial, and (b) resolving cases through judgments or resolution.

Deciding cases posed no problem to me. From my experience as a Hearing Officer of the Juvenile and Domestic Relations Court (JDRC) and later as Court Attorney in the office of a Supreme Court Justice, I had learned how to analyze and weigh evidence from where the facts are drawn and how to interpret and apply the proper law and jurisprudence to the case. The only problem in this aspect of our work is when the records are too voluminous, such that too much time is required to study the case.

What gave me the nerves early on was conducting hearings. This is because the judge faces the public, consisting of the prosecution or complainant's counsel, the defense and the litigants as well as all sorts of people from all walks of life who are involved or have interest in the cases calendared for the day. Here, the judge has to make snap decisions on every conceivable question brought in open court. The judge has to make rulings without having to refer to any book or other reference material; hence, a judge has to have the Rules of Court handy plus a general knowledge of all laws, some of which one never learned in law school.

Some lawyers try to impress the judge by talking too much, as if they know everything. Older lawyers are prone to intimidate the judge with their antics. There was one handsome lawyer who was winking at the judge while making a manifestation before the court, as if his good looks will make the judge succumb to his arguments. This judge just ignored him.

STENOGRAPHIC NOTES

All courts are courts of record; hence, all proceedings must have written transcripts. In making decisions, when citing statements made by a witness during a court hearing, I cite the date of the testimony and the particular page in the transcript of stenographic notes (TSN) where it is found. The statements made by witnesses must be faithfully and correctly quoted; otherwise, the context of their testimony may be altered.

But stenographic notes sometimes pose a problem. When there are many or long trials conducted in a day, the stenographer concerned finds it difficult to promptly transcribe his/her notes. As a result, the judge has no or incomplete TSN to rely on in making judgments. To remedy this, I devised my own transcribing system while conducting hearings, using abbreviations or signs for long words. Subsequently, my stenographers learned to borrow and rely on my notes to complete their TSN, even if they use tape recorders during hearings.

SENTENCING CRIMINALS

Whenever I promulgated judgments in criminal cases, my heart would beat faster and my hands would get cold and clammy, as if I was the one being sentenced. Curtailing the liberty of accused persons and incarcerating them for certain periods often gave me the feeling that I was cutting up their physical bodies.

Seeing the reactions of the accused and members of their family also made my heart bleed for them. Only the manifestation of defense counsel that they are going to appeal my decision normalizes my pulse rate. I welcome such appeals to make sure that I did not make a mistake in rendering judgments, especially in criminal cases. Fortunately or unfortunately, none of my judgments in criminal cases was reversed by the higher courts.

How much more nervous would I have felt if I had to impose the death penalty or at least life imprisonment? Thank God I had no chance to impose either one.

During the time I was a trial judge, the Constitution did not provide for the death penalty. Subsequently, when a Constitutional amendment opened the way for its imposition through an act of the legislature, I was already an appellate court justice. And the Rules of Court provides that upon the finding of guilt in capital offenses, the CA shall only make its judgment without sentencing, but will elevate the case to the Supreme Court for automatic review.

Even after the abolition of the death penalty through another act of Congress, the rule is that whenever the CA finds that life imprisonment or *reclusion perpetua* is imposable, it is supposed to elevate the case to the Supreme Court. It is thus the Supreme Court *en banc* which makes the final sentencing for capital offenses. I thank God that I was spared the ignominy of sentencing someone to death or depriving them their liberty for life.

[In civil cases, only two of my judgments in the entire 23 years that I served in the judiciary were reversed by the Supreme Court. Coincidentally, there were people trying to influence my decisions in such cases. Did they also do the same in the Supreme Court? Just thinking.)

My decisions rendered as a first-level court judge were all affirmed when appealed all the way up to the Court of Appeals (CA). On the other hand, of those I rendered as a Regional Trial Court judge, two were not totally affirmed on appeal: one was modified while the other was dismissed due to a procedural technicality and was not resolved on the merits of my judgment.

MARTIAL LAW VICTIMS

Among the cases I handled as a trial judge, I consider the case against certain military officials during the martial law years as one of the most difficult I have ever handled. These military officials were generally known to be abducting, torturing and/or killing people for any real or imagined reason — with impunity.

The case was filed by the victims who were unceremoniously arrested, detained and tortured for 2½ to 3 years. They were claiming damages against the military officers and their subordinates for the sufferings they experienced while in detention. But the defendants filed a motion to dismiss on the ground that damages may not be claimed during the time that the privilege of the writ of habeas corpus was suspended by the President, and that they could not be held liable for damages because they were only performing their official duties.

While the judge (Judge L) who was officially assigned to the case was on protracted leave of absence, the case was assigned to another judge (Judge F) in Quezon City. This substitute judge (Judge F) upheld the position of the defendants and dismissed the case. A Motion for Reconsideration (MR) was filed by the plaintiffs, but Judge F, without ruling on the MR, inhibited himself from the case. It was returned to the regular Judge (Judge L) when the latter reported back to office.

Judge L did not rule on the Motion for Reconsideration. Instead, he declared that the Order of Dismissal had already attained finality. His partiality was thus questioned, and he too had to recuse himself from the case.

If I was afraid of the general who had a case before me in my early days as a judge, I had more reason to fear repercussions in this case, where the defendants included the Chief of Staff of the Armed Forces of the Philippines — a well-known general whose loyalty and closeness to the former President was beyond question, plus several notorious colonels, lieutenants, sergeants and others who are generally known to be "hatchet men" during martial law.

But, horror of all horrors, the case was re-raffled to me!

I earnestly sought God's guidance on what to do, after which, I saw no point in the dismissal of the case. I granted the MR and ordered the reinstatement of the case. This was questioned before the Supreme Court, which sustained my resolution.

The case was then returned to me for trial on the merits. The plaintiffs' evidence was very convincing as to how the plaintiffs were arrested almost simultaneously in their different places of abode at night without any valid warrant, detained incommunicado in various military camps, deprived of their properties and personal effects, denied visits by their kin and lawyers, and tortured in various ways, usually while blindfolded, such as by repetitious beating, boxing, kicking, punching, stripping naked, pulling of hair or beard, pounding of head on the wall, stepping on the genitals or on the chest, electrocution of the genitals, burning of different parts of the body through lighted cigarettes, being forced to sign 'confessions' without being given a chance to read them, being threatened with death if they did not confess to being communists, and other inhuman or cruel punishment.

The Chief Physician of the Supreme Court Clinic who was directed to physically examine the complainants, testified as to the injuries she found on their bodies, thereby confirming the torture and physical sufferings inflicted upon them.

Before the defendants could start presenting their defense evidence, a complication arose when the trial was overtaken by the EDSA revolution, resulting in the disappearance of the defendants from their military offices. Communications to them were drastically cut, since their only addresses on record were their military offices.

The plaintiffs' counsel then moved that the case be deemed submitted for decision, praying that I render judgment solely on the basis of their evidence. They based their motion on the principle that once the court acquires jurisdiction over a case, that jurisdiction is never lost. And since the court had acquired jurisdiction over the persons of the defendants through the proper service of summons upon them, it devolved upon them to take note of the developments on the case, and their failure to appear should be considered as waiver of their right to present evidence on their behalf.

This time, I denied the plaintiffs' motion, ordering them to determine the present whereabouts of the defendants. We notified the immediate past Solicitor General who was the defendants' counsel, as well as the succeeding Solicitor General, but both denied representing or continuing to represent the defendants. I then ordered that the notice of hearing be published in a newspaper of general circulation, giving the defendants thirty (30) days to appear to manifest if they would present evidence on their behalf, and notifying them of the next date of hearing. When no one appeared for them, and upon plaintiffs' motion, I was constrained to render judgment against the defendants, except as to those who were not identified by the plaintiffs when they were blindfolded. I ordered the defendants to pay temperate, moral and exemplary damages plus attorney's fees to the plaintiffs who were able to testify and substantiate their contentions.

This judgment was hailed by the bar and the media as an act of courage. Former Senator Jovito R. Salonga, who became the first Chairman of the Presidential Commission on Good Government (PCGG), requested for several copies and brought them with him to the USA in his quest to recover the Marcoses' ill-gotten wealth.

CULTURE SHOCK

My staff in the CA, as well as those in the trial courts I served, were all trustworthy and dedicated. I considered anyone who leaves as a great loss to me. But I let them go when it is for their own good, such as for greener pastures or for convenience, especially for those who live so far away from my court.

One of my lawyers who sought to leave was Atty. Mel, who had served me faithfully since I was a trial judge in Quezon

City, starting as a stenographer until she became a lawyer and followed me to the CA. She learned that there was an opening for the position of Branch Clerk of Court in the RTC of Quezon City. It is a higher and permanent item, in contrast to her Court Attorney position in the CA, which is co-terminus to my term. The RTC of Quezon City is also closer to her home. So, when she sought permission to transfer, I gave her not only permission but also a recommendation and wished her well.

She was easily appointed to the position she sought. A few months later, she sent word through the other lawyers in my staff that she wanted to return to my office. As I had not yet found any replacement in view of my meticulous care in selecting my staff members, I asked her to come and reassure me that she sincerely wanted to come back.

She came posthaste. Without much ado, she said, *"Justice, I got a culture shock. Judge X is so different from you. If he is not conducting hearings, he is in his chambers, watching TV or entertaining visitors. He leaves to me the preparation of all orders and decisions without studying them. He just approves and signs my prepared drafts. What is worse, he sometimes asks me to reverse my prepared drafts after he had entertained some visitors, even against my findings and best research. I see visitors coming in with some gifts and leaving afterwards without them. This goes on almost everyday. I am so afraid, Justice. I cannot continue to work for him."*

I decided to rehire her. Judge X later died suddenly without being charged or found out about his shenanigans.

BOUNTIFUL HARVESTS

In 1989, I had a big surprise when Atty. Renato Callanta, a national officer of the Integrated Bar of the Philippines (IBP) came to visit me to inform me that I had been selected by the IBP as the Most Outstanding RTC Judge of the Philippines. There were five (5) nationally selected as outstanding judges for 1988 after a discreet observation and investigation, but I got the highest points, and was named Most Outstanding RTC Judge for 1988. The other RTC awardees were from Dagupan, Cebu, Manila and Zamboanga. Only one from the first level court,

Judge Thelma A. Ponferrada of the MetroTC of Manila, qualified for the award, although the IBP sought to award five. I learned that no other judge in Quezon City was nominated for the award.

The awarding ceremonies were covered by media and later published in the major dailies. The day after the event, I brought some snacks to the office for some of my colleagues who might come to congratulate me. No one came. Instead, the lawyers who appeared for hearing on that day were the ones who congratulated me in open court.

Actually, I had been receiving awards and citations from socio-civic organizations for my judiciary work as well for my extra-legal work for the welfare of children. Among those that gave awards were the Quezon City Youth Development Foundation, the YWCA of Quezon City, the Philippine Women Judges Association, the Quezon City Chapter of the IBP, etc. Unfortunately, I lost about eight of my plaques and citations when our office was gutted by fire in 1988.

I considered the IBP award as the most prestigious until 1992 when I got another award for Judicial Excellence as Outstanding RTC Judge from the Foundation for Judicial Excellence (FJE), which sought to encourage excellence in the judiciary by recognizing those who performed well.

This time, there were two awardees from the RTC aside from myself, namely, Judges Bernardo Pardo of Manila and Portia Hormacheulos of Cebu. Only one qualified from the first level court, the same Judge Ponferrada of Manila. As in the case of the IBP awards, I got the highest points and was again asked to deliver the response on behalf of all the awardees. The award carried a statuette plus cash prize of P50,000.00 and automatic recommendation to the next higher judicial post.

Judge Pardo was promoted to the CA that same year. In 1993, I was again nominated for one of the eight vacancies in the CA. Filtering reports had it that I started as No. 2 in Malacañang's short list of candidates, but I gradually dropped from second to 3rd, 4th, 5th, 6th, 7th and 8th. When I was hanging on in the No. 8 slot, someone from Malacañang called me to advise me to get a *padrino*, but I opted not to. I missed that promotion in 1993.

Some well-meaning friends who apparently were aware of my judicial record called to say that they were disappointed in not finding my name among the new appointees to the CA in 1993. Former Sen. Salonga scolded my sisters for not telling him about my nomination, while our then Congressman, Rep. Dante Liban, who I accidentally met at a function in Club Filipino, volunteered to help if I was nominated again.

In 1994, the Foundation for Judicial Excellence nominated me again for promotion to the CA. This time, Sen. Salonga's term in the Senate had expired. But he asked the Pastor of Cosmopolitan Church, Rev. Cirilo A. Rigos, to see then Sen. Leticia R. Shahani for an endorsement to President Fidel V. Ramos. Rev. Rigos obliged, but he told me afterwards not to hope because Sen. Shahani had already recommended 16 other people to the 9 vacant posts, and I would probably be the 17th. I did not hope anymore.

Surprisingly, I got the promotion to the CA in 1994. Unknown to me, some people gave good word for me. Among them were then Justice Flerida Ruth P. Romero of the Supreme Court and Vice Mayor Charito Planas of Quezon City. I learned about this when they congratulated me.

It is in the CA where I served the longest.

When I was the Chairperson of the 11th Division of the CA, and therefore No. 11 in the hierarchical ranking in the court, my sister-in-law, Leonor Magtolis Briones, who was then the National Treasurer, called me to ask if I wanted to be promoted to the Supreme Court. According to her, she thought of me because then President Joseph (Erap) Estrada told her that she was the only one in his Cabinet who had not asked him for anything. When the President bluntly asked her what it is that she wanted, she thought of me. That would have been a golden opportunity, but I did not want to jump ahead of those who were more senior to me in rank. So I declined the offer with thanks.

My colleagues who learned about this berated me for not taking advantage of that rare opportunity, which, they said was a "sure thing." They pointed out there are lower-ranking CA justices who had sought and have been appointed to the SC. And they are right because now, even those who are down the line in rank, *i.e.* not even a Division Chairman, had been elevated to the SC.

Erap's presidency prematurely ended and he had no more chance to consider me again. In any case, the Supreme Court, during that time, automatically recommended the five highest-ranking justices in the CA to the Judicial and Bar Council (JBC). The JBC is the body that screens applicants and recommends at least three candidates to any vacant judicial post to the President.

I was nominated at least four times, and recommended by the JBC to Malacañang twice, in one of which, I got the highest points in the JBC's scoreboard. But I never sought help from any influential people. Not surprisingly, I was never appointed to the Supreme Court, despite then President Gloria Arroyo's declaration that she would appoint the one who got the highest score in the JBC. But I have no regrets because my prayer has always been, *"Lord, if You want me there, I know You will find a way. May Your will be done."*

I got a final award when I retired from the CA. Having decided all my cases which had been submitted for decision, I was given an Achievement Award, another statuette with a cash prize of P100,000 by the CA. I happily donated the amount to my staff, without whom, I could not have earned that award.

જ જી

The Footprints I Had Left

On the occasion of my compulsory retirement on November 29, 2005, my daughter Grace, who was my Chief of Staff in the Court of Appeals, silently and single-handedly worked to produce a Souvenir Program. She asked some of those people with whom I had worked or been associated with, and the few lawyers she could contact who had cases before me, to write messages of good-bye. As far as I know, it was the first time that such a collection of messages was done for a retiring justice in the CA.

Here is what they said (the positions of the message-givers are as of November 29, 2005):

It is my pleasure to greet Justice Delilah V. Magtolis as she retires from the judiciary on November 29, 2005.

Justice Lily Magtolis and I, along with 7 others, joined the Court of Appeals in March 1994. On several occasions I had the privilege of working with her in some special divisions of the Court and I can state with certainty that Justice Lily, as we fondly call her, has sterling attributes of a first rate appellate magistrate, having a good grasp of both substantive and adjective laws and an exceptionally analytical mind that quickly lays hold of highly complicated factual situations, breaks and simplifies them and just as quickly applies to them pertinent statutes and case law.

Justice Lily possesses unimpeachable probity, integrity, and honesty. From the moment she joined the Court up to this day, she has remained simple, sincere and unaffected, for she says what she means and means what she says. And in all her *ponencias*, we can easily perceive the glorification and triumph of justice. And may I therefore add that Justice Lily's retirement will leave the Court a void that will be quite difficult to fill up.

Godardo A. Jacinto
Acting Presiding Justice, Court of Appeals

❧ ❦

You know a person by what she says, better still by what she does, best of all by what she is.

To me, Justice Delilah Vidallon-Magtolis is a quintessential jurist. In public and in private, she exemplifies propriety, always conscious of the ethical dimensions of her position. She is unassuming and lives the values and principles that make a lawyer just and a human being noble. Consistently, Justice Magtolis did her best to strengthen the rule of law, and immensely contributed to the public's high regard for the judiciary.

Mabuhay Justice Magtolis! I am certain you will continue to let your light shine before others and continue to serve country and humanity.

Atty. Lilia B. de Lima
Director General, Philippine Economic Zone Authority
President, Philippine Alumni Association of
the Academy of American and International Law

❧ ❦

Warm Greetings!

It gives me great pleasure to greet a fellow Caviteña and a judicial colleague, Justice Delilah V. Magtolis, on the occasion of her retirement from the Court of Appeals.

I have known her since the days of the Juvenile and Domestic Relations Court of Manila and have seen her climb up the judicial ladder, and most deservingly so. I recall that the late Justice Corazon Juliano Agrava was so impressed with her performance that she was one of those who spoke of her highly when she was considered for her first assignment in the Judiciary and later for the Court of Appeals.

I thank her most sincerely for being one with us in the cause of judicial education and for her unstinted cooperation as a Professorial Lecturer of the Philippine Judicial Academy.

I wish her all the best and more achievements even during her retirement, so that we may continue to benefit from her well-known capabilities and her wide experience as a jurist, as a lecturer, and a mover.

Justice Ameurfina A. Melencio Herrera
Supreme Court (Ret.)
Chancellor, Philippine Judicial Academy

❦

More than three years ago, that is, on July 23, 2002, former Secretary of Justice Sedfrey Ordoñez and I sent to the Chairman and Members of the Judicial and Bar Council the Monitoring and Evaluation by *Bantay Katarungan* Student Monitors – who had been selected for their competence, idealism and moral integrity – the following excerpts from the evaluation report of applicant Justice Delilah Magtolis for one of the two vacancies in the Supreme Court:

". . very competent and extremely hard working. . . a silent worker who never entertains 'follow ups' of decisions.

*Her colleagues in the Court of Appeals who were interviewed
consider her as 'beyond reproach.' Her independence of
mind and moral courage deeply impressed our student
monitors and supervising lawyers. (Specific examples
omitted). Like Justice Callejo, Justice Magtolis does not
approach JBC members, Supreme Court justices, or VIPs.
Because of her unassailable competence, moral integrity,
independence of mind and moral courage, she deserves to be
in the Supreme Court."*

The JBC, to our knowledge, recommended her to the
President for appointment to the Supreme Court, but
unfortunately Justice Magtolis was not appointed. Like Federal
Judge Learned Hand of the 2nd Circuit Court of Appeals who
came very close to being appointed due to his exceptional
standards for "clarity of expression and judicial craftsmanship,"
it is the High Court's loss, but the continuing gain of the
Court of Appeals that Justice Magtolis has remained where she
continues to be the bearer of the light. Now that she is about
to retire, we in *Bantay Katarungan* are partly happy for the rest
she will richly deserve but partly sad for the impending loss of
the Court of Appeals.

Jovito R. Salonga
Former Senate President
Founder, Bantay Katarungan

❧ ❧

Justice Delilah Vidallon-Magtolis enjoys a solid reputation
for her unsullied integrity, depth of character and
uncompromising independence. She personifies truth and
fairness, decisiveness and on-time performance.

Her decision are well-crafted. They reflect an analytical
and a logical mind, bound by strict ethical standards. Her
language is elegant, stirring and grammatical; her style, consistent
and easy-to-understand.

Her virtuous upbringing and spiritual anchor made her an ideal judge, a perfect model of justice personified.

Justice Artemio V. Panganiban
Supreme Court

❧ ❧

Justice "Lily" is the epitome of an ideal member of the Judiciary. She is hardworking, conscientious and dedicated to every task she undertakes. True to what her nickname symbolizes, her integrity is beyond reproach, a quality that everyone in the Judiciary should emulate.

Justice Ma. Alicia Austria-Martinez
Supreme Court

❧ ❧

The judiciary and the public shall be unhappy with the compulsory retirement of Justice Delilah V. Magtolis from the Court of Appeals. For 23 years, she has served as an exemplary magistrate, quietly discharging her duties with unfailing integrity, competence and efficiency. We shall also certainly miss her steadfast sense of "delicadeza", a trait that seems to have generally receded from the public service.

Alfredo L. Benipayo
Solicitor General

❧ ❧

The judiciary has a gem in Justice Delilah whose impeccable integrity, proven competence and independence, and consummate industry capture the qualities of an ideal public servant.

I am happy to have been with her in the "Cloud 9" batch of appointees to the Court of Appeals in March 1994.

As she performs her swan song today, I take pleasure in congratulating her for a job well done and wishing her continued health and happiness.

Justice Conchita Carpio Morales
Supreme Court

∽ ∾

Retirements are both sad and happy occasions. Sad – because it means a parting of professional ways; happy – because retirement brings a new phase in the retiree's life, and perhaps doubly happy, too, because one gets a chance to hear the accolades and wonderful remarks of friends and colleagues in the profession while one is still robust and kicking.

Justice Magtolis is a true friend. And it is not just a matter of courtesy that I say that. She is a friend in the word's true sense: ready to extend a helping hand and a listening ear even when she may be quite busy with work or with concerns of her own. I am certain that many other individuals – both from the judiciary and within Justice Magtolis' other circles – have benefited from such sharing of her "anatomical appendages."

As to our honoree's professional virtues, I can attest to her intelligence, her uncommon zeal for hard work, her diligence and, of course, her unquestionable integrity. These are ethical standards that are getting rare as gems, but which shine with luster from Justice Magtolis' works, judicial and non-judicial. Her exit from the judicial world will certainly make a difference henceforth.

Despite these glittering qualities, however, Justice Magtolis remains garbed in simplicity. There is no air about her, and this is what makes her all the more worthy of note and emulation.

No other fitting send-off words can be given her, except that may God's choicest blessings continue to be with her as she traverses this new road in her life!

Justice Minita V. Chico-Nazario
Supreme Court

అల స్

The curtain is about to come down on the distinguished career of an illustrious former colleague in the Court of Appeals whom I had the fortune of working with for nearly a decade.

"Lily", as I and my former colleagues in the appellate court fondly address Madame Justice Delilah Vidallon-Magtolis, is a remarkable lady jurist. She swaps jokes with abundance and infectious laughter, the same abundance of serious thoughts and ideas when questions of law are on the table.

During all the time that I worked with her in the Court of Appeals, first as an Associate Justice and later as its Presiding Justice, I have always found Lily to be an amiable friend, quick in jests and humorous repartee, yet commanding respect by all her peers. She inspired those around her with her work ethics, professionalism, easy wit and most of all, kindness.

I join my former colleagues in the appellate court in wishing you, Lily, good health and all the happiness you richly deserve as you begin a new journey in life. Your retirement from the Bench would be a big loss for the Judiciary but an enormous gain for your family and loved ones.

With all my best wishes!

Justice Cancio P. Garcia
Supreme Court

అల స్

Excellence comes naturally to Lily Magtolis. Whether it is crafting a decision, performing an assigned task or serving in the House of the Lord, one is certain that this will be accomplished with fidelity, integrity and finesse. This I experienced in full measure when we worked closely together to arrange an international conference of the Philippine Women Judges Association (PWJA). As President of the organization, I merely laid down in broad strokes what was expected of Lily in her key position and she executed these meticulously to the minutest detail, not even disdaining to walk the extra mile.

Because she imposes exacting standards on herself, she expects no less from others. So upright is she that she will not brook any unethical or dishonest behavior from colleagues and staff. Of a cheerful, vivacious disposition, she evokes a similar response from those she deals with.

No mere "Lily of the Valley," she has soared to the mountaintops on "wings of song" accompanied by devoted husband Gani and accomplished daughters Gail, Joy and Grace.

I am grateful for this singular privilege of being able to contribute a word portrait of a wonderful, warm person and a fine Christian lady.

Justice Flerida Ruth Romero (Ret.)
Supreme Court

Mme. Justice Magtolis' retirement leaves a void. Throughout her judicial career which spanned a period of 23 years, she earned a reputation for efficiency, industry and independence worthy of emulation. As she moves on to a well-deserved liberation from the burdens of a magistrate, I wish her the best and hope that her successor will perpetuate her work ethic and her single-minded devotion to the public trust that attaches to the judicial office she occupied with honor.

Justice Minerva Gonzaga-Reyes (Ret.)
Supreme Court

The retirement of Madam Justice Delilah Vidallon-Magtolis brings to a close the dedicated and upright service of one of the most admired jurists of the Court of Appeals. She is a person with rare courage and firm commitment to uphold at all times the integrity and dignity of the legal profession. She gives hope to our younger generation that justice, truth and the rule of law will always prevail. Her many *ponencias* speak of her rigorous brainwork and moral authority. Her unblemished reputation which she has maintained till the end of her days in the judiciary and her honored name are the most precious legacies which she leave to her children and her children's children.

I am proud to be counted one among her many friends for she is sincere, loyal and honest in all her dealings.

Justice Eugenio S. Labitoria
Court of Appeals

ও ৩

Cloud Nine. That was the appellation I gave in good humor to the second and biggest batch of appointees of President Fidel Ramos to this Appellate Court – Justices Barcelona, Hofileña, Jacinto, Labitoria, Magtolis, Morales, Reyes, Vasquez, Salas. The ranking appears alphabetized save for the last name. The appointment was made in February, but we took our oath in March, 1994. For a month, we were on suspended animation, teetering on the short list of thirty-six. Every year, since then, we never fail to celebrate with thanksgiving the event that started to bind us together.

One is now in the High Court – Justice Morales. Three have earlier retired – Barcelona, Hofileña and Salas. Before the year ends, two more will reach the mandatory age of retirement – Magtolis this November 29, followed by Labitoria on December 13. That will leave only three of us in this Court – Jacinto, Reyes and Vasquez – all candidates for Presiding Justice (PJ) as of this writing mid-November.

Lily, as Justice Delilah Vidallon Magtolis is fondly called, would have been again a strong contender for PJ. But the age barrier has caught up with her. Concededly, she has the drive and diligence, the leadership abilities, the vim and vitality and the mold of a good head of an office. She can still have that privilege, probably in the academe, having been a former trustee of the Philippine Christian University. A person of her caliber and credentials, integrity and intelligence, will always be an asset in any organization or sphere of work. It is easy to predict that another window of opportunity is bound to open and welcome this talented lady to a new world of endeavor.

On lecturing, we have been paired more than once by the UP Law Center and the Philippine Judicial Academy. In Isabela, sometime ago, she was a hit on Family Law while I shared my bit on Special Penal Laws. In Lucena, just recently, we both served as resource speakers on the Code of Conduct for Court Personnel. We alternately zeroed in on fidelity to duty, confidentiality, conflict of interest and performance of duties. Ethics is one topic close to her heart and it is very fitting that she has been the unchallenged chair of the CA Ethics Committee for a long while till she retires.

Her two-syllabic monicker aptly describes her: she is pure and simple, fair and faithful. Unlike her namesake in the Bible who betrayed Samson to the Philistines, our Delilah is loyal and dedicated to her family, to her faith, to her profession and to the cause of justice. One can be sure she will always stand up to be counted for what she believes in. She wavers not nor moves away from a principled encounter. But she is never belligerent. For what she cannot win by argument she can win by her music. She sings well and even does better on the organ and the piano, with or without the music sheets. Armed with glittering eyes, she can strike a pleasant dialogue and leave you light-hearted after a day of hard wok.

Justice Ruben T. Reyes
Court of Appeals

It has been said that the most beautiful of flowers are to be found on the highest mountain tops and nestled in the most secluded valleys. We are lucky that we need not trek far and wide to search for the mountain lily because there is one such enthralling and lovely bloom among us – our very own Lily.

A woman of noble character is worth far more than rubies (Proverbs 31:10). Lily is such a woman. She fears the Lord and seeks His wisdom in everything than she does, which is evident from her *ponencias,* speeches and actions as they reflect sound judgment and discernment.

Lily is a great blessing to her family and friends. I am privileged and honored to be among her friends.

Justice Marina L. Buzon
Court of Appeals

With the retirement of Senior Associate Justice Delilah Vidallon-Magtolis on November 29, 2005, she will end a distinguished career in the judiciary. She has served the judiciary with competence, honor, and integrity.

I fondly remember her as my former Chairman who commended me for a thorough and well-researched review of one case, the ponencia of which was personally written by me.

Justice Magtolis would have been an ideal Presiding Justice but as a colleague would describe her later, Justice Magtolis is the best PJ who never was. We praise her virtues as an ideal magistrate and I am sure that we will miss Justice Magtolis for her competence, industry and integrity.

Justice Rodrigo V. Cosico
Court of Appeals

The name of Justice Delilah (which in Hebrew means "delicate") must have been taken from the Holy Bible by her parents. As you know there was a time when ancient Israel was ruled by the judges, and one of the more notable of these judges was the Danite Samson. Samson had earlier dallied with two Philistine women, but his meretricious affair with the third Philistine woman Delilah (she who was called the woman from the Valley of Sorek), proved his final undoing.

In more modern times and particularly in the Court of Appeals of the Republic of the Philippines, we also have our own version of Delilah- Madame Justice Delilah V. Magtolis; and Madame Justice Delilah Vidallon Magtolis, as her Hebrew name suggests, is indeed "delicate" in her judicial function. She is a silent worker, and like silent water that runs deep, she is a reticent and unobtrusive, if an effective and efficient performer and achiever. And, also like the Biblical Delilah who destroyed the nemesis of her people, the mighty Samson, our very own Madame Justice Delilah totally annihilated the nemesis of the clogged court docket: her judicial case load.

Madame Justice Delilah is not only a topnotch jurist but is also a musical artist par excellence. She has always been an active participant in the Court of Appeals cultural and social activities where she had had ample opportunities to display her outstanding musical endowments. Very few justices indeed, here and elsewhere, have such an exceptional talent for music, the language of the soul, as she. And it is no exaggeration to say that she could have attained brilliant success as a concert pianist, as much as a stand-out lawyer and judge that she is. St. Cecilia, the patroness of music and another Sagittarian (whose birthday, by the way on November 22, comes just a week before her own), must have been playing the piano for her when she was born. She will be sorely missed in the cultural and social activities of the Court.

Madame Justice Delilah's exit from the portals of this Court is like the closing of the doors of a great cathedral. Whence comes another?

Justice Renato C. Dacudao
Court of Appeals

Justice Lily was my boss when I was a law clerk at the Supreme Court. Like the morning lily, she came as a pleasing sight and a delightful fragrance to her subordinates and peers who were always refreshed by her amiable presence every working day of the week. As fate had it, we would later meet here as fellow Justices of the Court of Appeals.

She is not only a well-respected Justice but is also a brilliant educator, an eloquent writer, a sincere and trusted friend, genuinely pious, compassionate, and God-loving person. I know of only three doors in which Justice Lily frequents and these are, the door to their house, the door to her office and the door to the church.

Justice Lily is the type that would rather seek happiness in the lap and love of her family, in the company of her inspirational books, in the wholesome occupations of her idyllic home, and in the pious affairs of her church. She belongs to that rare few who has successfully resisted the obdurate pressures of work and has crafted that delicate balance which enables her to keep a very happy and close-knit family and a fortified and solid relationship with God.

Justice Remedios Salazar-Fernando
Court of Appeals

❧ ❧

Having been with this Court for more than six (6) years, I must say that it was not difficult for me to have come to admire Justice Lily Vidallon Magtolis. Perhaps it was not so much as her having a keen mind and legal acumen, but more so because of her being humble, good mannered and God-fearing.

As my Division Chairperson for quite a time, it was indeed educational and a privilege to have observed at close range not only her judicial expertise but also her devotion and dedication to serve the ends of justice and the rule of law. Her faithfulness to God is undoubtedly the reason for her unblemished reputation and unassailable integrity.

Indeed, as shared by not just a few, it is a pity that she was never given the opportunity to be elevated to the Highest Tribunal of the land where she would have been a great and welcomed addition.

> **Justice Jose L. Sabio, Jr.**
> Court of Appeals

ৰ্ঞ ঔ

It is always heartwarming to be given the honor to work with Justice Delilah Vidallon Magtolis whose most remarkable and highly distinguished record and exemplary performance in the legal profession has not only enriched this great institution, but also laid down the red carpet for us who follow.

This Honorable Lady who had pledged more than four (4) decades of her life to decline no combat to be able to serve and promote a just and humanitarian society, has indeed proven herself a worthy partner of the government in nation-building. She should be a timely inspiration for all of us as guardians of justice.

> **Justice Bienvenido L. Reyes**
> Court of Appeals

ৰ্ঞ ঔ

An anecdote is told about 2 great legal minds known for their nobility in spirit. Then Senior Associate Justice of the Supreme Court Roberto Concepcion wanted to yield to then Associate Justice J.B.L. Reyes so that he instead could become the Chief Justice before the latter retires. J.B.L. Reyes however, declined this honor to give regard to the former's seniority, thus making Justice Concepcion succeed Chief Justice Caesar Bengzon.

In the Court of Appeals, I have not known of a lady justice who approximates these two honorable men other than Justice Delilah Vidallon-Magtolis. In 1999-2000 when there was an existing vacancy in the Supreme Court, former National Treasurer Leonor Briones (a sister-in-law) enticed Justice Lily to grab this golden opportunity and apply for the position. But she readily gave a thumbs down to the offer as she thought it improper and insensitive to bypass the senior justices of the Court of Appeals. In a world full of people with the natural propensity for career advancement and prestige, some of whom will do almost everything to get ahead, Justice Lily shone in showing one and all her ethical moorings – her *delicadeza* – which I find very rare nowadays.

To me, she is the best Presiding Justice that the Court unfortunately never had. The antithesis of the Bible's Delilah, she is all heart, an incarnation of all that is good – motherly, pure to the bone, principled, completely honest, charming with a disarming smile, forgiving, approachable, friendly, talented, pragmatic and very intelligent. Also noted for her gentleness, I bet that during her days as a judge, she may have conversed with a contrite and broken accused in this manner.

"Have you ever been sentenced to imprisonment?

"No, your Honor," said the prisoner who burst into tears.

"There, there, don't cry," said the kind Judge Lily, "You're going to be now..."

I could only wish that my son could find a mother-in-law like her.

Justice Mariano C. Del Castillo
Court of Appeals

๏๛

Justice Lily is dedicated, fair, just, upright and a competent public servant whose reputation is beyond reproach. But more than all these, she is a devout woman of faith with no mean bone in her body.

Justice Josefina Guevara-Salonga
Court of Appeals

❧ ❧

A loyal friend with whom I have shared friends and moments of fun and discovery. A model jurist who has literally risen from the ranks in the bench, she is well-admired and well-respected by her colleagues for her unsoiled integrity and uncompromising dignity and for the logic and clarity of her *ponencias*. But for the unsound Constitutional provision that now compels her to retire from the second highest Court of the land, her honest toil, her commitment to the cause of justice and her abiding fidelity to law could have been fittingly capped with an ascent to the apex of the judicial hierarchy.

May she enjoy her retirement in blissful contentment with her family.

Justice Rebecca de Guia-Salvador
Court of Appeals

❧ ❧

A lady justice with integrity, independence of mind, courage and substance who will not hesitate to voice her piece not only in the adjudication of cases but also on matters that pertain to the interest and welfare of the court. She shall certainly be missed.

Justice Edgardo F. Sundiam
Court of Appeals

❧ ❧

It was an enriching experience for me to have worked with her as our Chairman of the Fifth Division, with Justice Jose L. Sabio, Jr. as senior member and myself as junior member. A God-fearing person, she is also approachable and understanding. As a jurist, she is not only knowledgeable, but also open-minded, tolerant of other's views and independent in her judgment. She is highly respected by her peers — a truly remarkable lady. If only she is not required by law to retire from the service, she could still very well serve the Court.

On the occasion of her retirement, we wish her Godspeed and many enjoyable years with her family and friends.

Justice Hakim S. Abdulwahid
Court of Appeals

∽

Justice Magtolis is a very meticulous, very perceptive and very exacting jurist. She is sensitive to criticism and admires excellence in work.   But she is very friendly and a very understanding individual. It is an honor to know her as a former colleague in the Regional Trial Court of Quezon City and later as my chairman in the Sixth Division in the Court of Appeals. We won't miss her too much because her legacy will stay.

Justice Noel G. Tijam
Court of Appeals

∽

I personally know Justice Delilah Vidallon-Magtolis because of the many years we worked together in the Supreme Court under Chief Justice Felix V. Makasiar. Fortunately, with my promotion to the Court of Appeals, we were together again. During those years, I witnessed how dedicated Justice Lily (as she is fondly called) Magtolis is in the different roles she performs in life. I can say that she is an ideal public servant. She is a hardworking lady with high integrity who always puts God in the center of all the things she does.

She is equally devoted as a wife and mother of three children that I have seen grow under her loving care. A few years back, she and her husband Gani celebrated their 40th wedding anniversary. It was truly an admirable sight to see how an achiever in her career can be so successful also in her family life. Justice Lily Magtolis takes time out from her busy schedule to make sure her children are taken care of well not only physically but more so emotionally and spiritually under her guidance and supervision. It is no wonder then that Lily and Gani were able to raise children who are God-loving and well-rounded professionals.

As a colleague, I find her very thoughtful, always thinking about the welfare of others, especially the lowly employees and poor people. We will always remember Lily for her sense of dedication and fairness in her work and relationships with people. Lastly, we will remember with fondness her talents in music that she most generously shared with us in many of our gatherings.

Justice Jose C. Reyes, Jr.
Court of Appeals

ৡ৯

Justice Delilah Vidallon-Magtolis is a classic model of the blind-folded lady bearing a sword and a scale. She is known for her quiet humility and a sense of justice that is guided by a deep understanding of human nature and frailties.

The light cast in the judicial firmament by Justice Magtolis or Lily, as she is fondly called by her friends and associates, is manifested by the numerous awards and citations she received from the public and private sectors of our society.

With her retirement, Justice Lily will be sorely missed. May God bless her with good health and happiness always!

Justice Aurora Santiago-Lagman
Court of Appeals

❧ ❧

I first met Justice Magtolis when I, as a Solicitor in the Office of the Solicitor General, appeared in her sala in RTC-Quezon city in a naturalization case. Needless to say, I was impressed by the way she conducted the trial. She was strict but fair, and while she was the type who would brook no nonsense from the lawyers appearing before her, she was always respectful in dealing with them. In just two settings, the hearing was terminated, and in less than a month, there was already a decision. No wonder, she had established a reputation for efficiency and competence, marked by unquestionable integrity, throughout her career in government service. Indeed, not only is she the perfect magistrate – erudite, dedicated, honest and just, with a special concern for children and the youth; as a person, she is warm, bright, pious, humble and sincere, with natural poise, refinement and grace. Indeed, a role model for Filipino women.

Justice Magdangal M. de Leon
Court of Appeals

❧ ❧

To be a member of the judiciary was a dream that proved to be the wisdom of her choice and now that she is retiring, it is to become the splendid reminder of her brilliant career.

To Justice Delilah Magtolis, this is the origin of a new beginning.

As a judge and then Justice of the Court of Appeals, she consistently demonstrated a high level of magisterial loyalty to her oath, speaking to the public only through her written decisions after exploring the issues at hand.

As a long-time colleague in the Regional Trial Court and in the Appeals Court, I stand high to exalt her for her deeds even as she approaches the promise of a more serene and blissful life.

Justice Monina A. Zenarosa
Court of Appeals

~ ~

I met Lily Magtolis through a mutual friend long before we found ourselves together in the Court of Appeals. She has impressed me as a very sincere person, humble, and steadfastly righteous in her convictions. She is truly a woman of intelligence & integrity worthy of appointment to the second highest court of the land. Her retirement leaves a wide void in the administration of justice in this country.

Presiding Justice Salome A. Montoya (Ret.)
Court of Appeals

~ ~

The retirement of Justice Delilah Magtolis will be a great loss to the judiciary for not only is she most qualified and dedicated, her honesty and integrity are unquestionable. Lily is well liked and highly respected by her peers and members of the Court. A loss indeed, but perhaps a gain for the academe?

All the best.

Presiding Justice Jesus M. Elbinias (Ret.)
Court of Appeals

To my dear friend Justice Lily:

You will be a great loss to the judiciary come your retirement on November 29, 2005. Your chances to be a Presiding Justice of the Court of Appeals or a member of the Supreme Court were taken away from you for reasons only GOD knows. I believe it's destiny. You will have more time for your better half, Engr. Gani and your family.

But, as a pillar in the judiciary, I honestly believe that come your retirement, PHILJA will definitely need your services for you are top in competence, honesty and integrity.

Justice Bennie A. Adefuin-de la Cruz (Ret.)
Court of Appeals

༻ ༺

It is my good fortune to have been associated with Justice Delilah Vidallon-Magtolis even only because we were appointed to the Court of Appeals together with the rest of the "Cloud 9 justices". Throughout these years, she has become the rock on which the Court stands. Her irrefutable competence, steadfast adherence to the law, and shining integrity, have indelibly stamped her with the mark of a modal magistrate of the court, of any Court.

Justice Hector L. Hofileña (Ret.)
Court of Appeals

༻ ༺

Justice Delilah Vidallon-Magtolis' forty-five year stint in the government service, 23 years of which she unflaggingly devoted to the Judiciary, provides a thoughtful and invigorating account of a public servant's life that is both exemplary and worth emulating.

Madame Magtolis epitomizes Mr. Chief Justice Hilario G. Davide's vision for a judiciary that is independent, effective, efficient and worthy of public trust and confidence.

Even a careless reading of the involvement of Justice Delilah Vidallon-Magtolis in both the legal academe and the Judiciary will push one to say that she fashioned a fabled career that can be said in one singularly powerful word – meritocracy.

Her Honor's retirement is one time when a person, friend or foe, will find it engaging to stop the power of prose and poetry that portray her life as a natural academician and her love for jurisprudential excellence.

Madame Justice Magtolis, to be certain will retire. I wonder how one retires from a regime of meritocracy.

Justice Raoul V. Victorino (Ret.)
Sandiganbayan
Member, Judicial & Bar Council

ശ്ശഃ

Justice Magtolis, we, your Court of Appeals family, will truly miss you.

We will remember your modest and amiable ways, your soft spot for the lowly employees, your unquestionable integrity, your dedication to and pride in your judicial calling.

Another thing that I will often be reminded of, long after you're gone, is your frugality where the Court's resources are concerned. When finally you opted to move to a better room, the one you had vacated and used without fanfare for many years required no less than a major renovation which the then Presiding Justice had no recourse but to approve, seeing how its appearance had lagged far behind those of your colleagues. Trappings do not mean much to you, as long as you can work in peace and quiet. You are unique in this sense, and I salute you.

Take care and God bless.

Atty. Tessie Gatmaitan
Clerk of Court
Court of Appeals

Justice Delilah (Lily) is a constant spray of womanliness in every turf where the wind of life settles her. Even in an institution where strictures are traditionally in place, she still radiates her inner self out into the open.

Her countenance readily unfolds a being that knows and extends none but warmth and genuine friendliness. But beyond and more than that, a deep sense of Christian purpose is discernible in her every word, in her every action. She walks the talk, and leads by her deed.

One need only take a leaf from her tome of achievements to see that her truly worthy concerns as a person permeate and characterize every aspect of her life, public as well as private.

A heralded accomplishment she has chalked up is her involvement in the protection and advancement of the interests, rights and welfare of the child. She has consistently invited attention to the vulnerability of the youth to undue pressure and even abuse in the course of that crucial stage of development to adulthood. She has urged positive action to provide the proper and encouraging environment for the growth of the child into manhood and womanhood.

Despite her refreshing humility and self-effacing personality, her achievements have not gone unnoticed, witnessed by numerous honors and awards she has received for her outstanding performance in the course of her stint in the bench. Her integrity has remained unassailed and her devotion to duty cannot be questioned. She is truly a woman and a jurist of substance.

Atty. Ofelia "Baby" Calcetas-Santos
President, FAIRchild

The heights by great men reached and kept
Were not attained by sudden flight,
But they, while their companions slept,
Were toiling upward and in the night.

— Henry Wadsworth Longfellow —

If there is one trait I could best describe our Honoree and Retiring Justice, it is her total dedication to duty.

When she was newly appointed Presiding Judge of the Metropolitan Trial Court of Quezon City in the 80's, I could not forget it was only her Court that conducted trial on a Holy Wednesday. The whole eighth floor of the Quezon City Hall was empty except her courtroom and her staff's office as she heard a party's application for a preliminary mandatory injunction. In the morning, she received the applicant's evidence. In the afternoon, she received the defendant's evidence. She adjourned shortly before 3:00 p.m. But by 4:30 p.m., her staff promulgated and released her order. There were no computers then yet.

Her dedication and industry did not wane a bit even as she was elevated as Regional Trial Court Judge of Quezon City. Among our ranks of Quezon City law practitioners, she is known for her straight-forwardness, honesty, competence and above all her sincere dedication to the cause of Justice and Truth.

We, in the practice of law, will surely miss Mme. Justice Delilah Vidallon-Magtolis as she retires from the bench today.

Atty. Ricardo J.M. Rivera
Practicing Attorney
President, UE Law Alumni

Justice Magtolis is – and was – a role model for all of us women lawyers. She is a role model for the judiciary. Honest. Straight as an arrow. Yet sympathetic, empathetic, and considerate. She did not have to be "trained" to be a Family

Court Judge. Her heart and soul were merged in her role as arbiter in sometimes bitter family disputes – allowing all parties dignity in their quest for justice. May your tribe increase, Justice Magtolis.

God blessed us with you.

Atty. Katrina Legarda
Practicing Attorney

ॐ ॐ

In a nutshell, Justice Delilah V. Magtolis, or simply "Lily" to her loved ones and close friends, is truly the essence of the rare and lovely flower.

As an Associate Justice of this Court, she has always taken pride in her good name and reputation. Her God-loving and God-fearing character is always evident in her steadfast commitment to the often difficult task of dispensing justice.

As an esteemed colleague, she has always extended a ready and eager hand to the endeavors of the Court and has constantly exhibited her unwavering support to all its programs aimed toward the better administration of justice.

But best of all, as a dear friend, I am very much in awe at her simplicity. And while her gentle and mild-mannered ways are some of her endearing traits, we will surely miss her hearty laughter at gatherings and fellowships among magistrates and acquaintances. She is indeed, in the truest sense of the word, what we affectionately call a *"totoong tao."*

Justice Conrado M. Vasquez, Jr.
Court of Appeals

ॐ ॐ

The quintessential Delilah Vidallon Magtolis is a multifaceted person – wife, mother, lawyer, jurist, public servant, feminist, child advocate, musician! Equipped with an inquisitive courageous mind and a firm set of spiritual values, she has consistently resisted the inclination to apply law in a purely formalistic manner ("slot-machine application," says Pound) and has shown a deep sensitivity for the effect of her decisions on others — a consistent display of the ethic of "caring" for others, as what the philosopher Levinas instructs. Quite a tough act to follow.

It is therefore difficult to believe, and for that matter, accept, that Justice Lily is retiring from the judiciary. I simply cannot conceive of the Philippine judiciary without a Justice Lily in it. For judicial service has been her commitment – her entire life – benchmarked by a high degree of independence, impartiality, fairness and competence. Having first met Justice Lily, an RTC Judge in Quezon City, in my early days of law practice, it was when I joined the bench in the late 80's that I came to know her as a person and cherish her, as I always will, as a valued friend.

We cannot hold back time and deny Justice Lily her hard earned right to spend more time with her loved ones, kith and kin, or venture into new worlds denied her by the demands of her judicial work. And we certainly cannot stop her from asking, in her moments of solitude savoring her new freedom:

"Oh, must we dream our dreams
And have them too? And have we room
for one more folded sunset, still quite warm?"

Zenaida E. Elepano
Court Administrator, Supreme Court

∾∾

Published by a Self-Publisher

Tatay Jobo Elizes was born in Manila, Philippines, in 1934, retiree, now based in NY, busy writing and self-publishing as a hobby and involved in piglets dispersal programs for livelihood projects in the Philippines via the internet.

ISBN-13-978: 1484020944   *ISBN-10:* 1484020944

Book List - Contact:
job_elizes@yahoo.com - tatay@usa.com

Writings 1 Book, 2012 + + 1. Obit, *Bambi Harper* + + 2. Speech, UP, 2003, *Butch Jimenez* + + 3. Speech, Silliman U, 2006, *Butch Jimenez* + + 4. The Mission Moment, *Dr. Phil Stack* + + 5. Subanon Spirits of Rice & Land - *Noel Cornel Alegre* + + 6. I Look Out The Window - *Atty. Toto Causing* + + 7. Ride On A Bus, Poem, *Melanie Ferrer, et al* + + 8. Why Am I Doing This, *Susie Barbieri* + 9. How To Court A Philippine Lady, *Rodel Ramos, et al* + + 10. Story of Bacna Surgical Mission, *Sylvia Salvador* + + 11. Catch That Story, *Tatay Jobo Elizes*

Writings 2 Book, 2012 + + 1. There Is Hope For The Philippines, *Grace Padaca* + + 2. Pointers On Employment Abroad, *Melanie Aquino* + + 3. Without KNCHS: (Love story), *Atty. Toto Causing* + + 4. 422 Years Ago, *Rodel Rodis* + + 5. Filipino American History Month, *Rodel Rodis* + + 6. A Need For Reflection, Gloom, *Cesar Torres* + + 7. Did Ninoy Die For Nothing, *Joey Concepcion* + + 8. Criteria - American Institute of Philanthropy, *Charity Guidelines (Feature)* + + 9. Coming Revolution In The Ballot, *Cesar Lumba* + + 10. 2009, A Retrospective, *Cesar Lumba* + + 11. Strangers In Our Own Country, *Casiano Mayor Jr.* + + 12. The Gypsy Soul, *Casiano Mayor Jr.* + + 13. An End To Cheating, *Sonny Coloma* + + 14. Toward Culture of Giving, Not Having, *Sonny Coloma* + + 15. 100 Reasons to be Proud as Pinoys, *Anonymous*

Writings 3 Book, 2010 + + I. EPIC25, Emerging Philippines Investors Coalition, *Norman Madrid* + + II. **Management Ability As An Issue,** *Dr. Rene B. Azurin* + + III. **Do We Really Want To Give Our Politicos More Power,** *Dr. Rene B. Azurin* + + IV. **Will 2010 Fulfill High Hopes For Better Life,** *Ernie D. Delfin* + + V. **Comelec Is The Root Of All Evils,** *Toto Causing* + + VI. **Advantages of Federalism / Parliamentary,** *Dr. Jose Abueva* + + VII. **Sometimes A Great Nation,** *Mar-Vic Cagurangan* + + VIII. **Great Conspiracy,** *Mar-Vic Cagurangan* + + IX. **Of Speech & Life's Riddles,** *Casiano Mayor* + + X. **Bad Start To The Year,** *Rod Garcia* + + XI. **A Dinner Out,** *Rod Garcia* + + XII. **One More Time,** *Roy Gaane* + + XIII. **Musings,** *Ceres Busa* + + XIV. **Value Formation For Good Citizenship,** *Roger Reyes, JMC Nepomuceno, Ramon Gonzales, CDVictory, Mila Marzo* + + XV. **On Being Filipino American,** *John Reyes* + + XVI. **The Monterey Peninsula,** *John Reyes* + + XVII. **The Salaza Fiesta,** *John Reyes* + + XVIII. **Salawikain: Filipino Proverbs,** *John Reyes* + + XIX. **Musikero (The Musician),** *John Reyes* + + XX. **Strange Noises,** *Tatay Jobo Elizes*

Writings 4 Book, 2010 + + I. **The State of Our Nation and Democracy In 2010: Building 'The Good Society" We Want,** *Dr. Jose V. Abueva* + + II. **Assessing Expanded Role of AFP in Nation Building,** *Col.Dennis Acop, Ret.* + + III. **Assessing RP's Security Strategies Alternative Views,** *Col. Dennis Acop, Ret.* + + IV. **The Way We Were,** *Fred Natividad* + + V. **Veterans of Ipo Dam, A Fiction,** *Fred Natividad* + + VI. **A Plea,** *Miguel Reyes Reynaldo* + + VII. **Int'l Youth Bowling, My Impressions,** *Marjorie Ann Elizes Reyes* + + VIII. **Mi Ultimo Adios (My Last Farewell),** *Dr. Jose P. Rizal* + + IX. **Aling Pagibig Sa Tinubuang Bayan,** *Gat. Andres Bonifacio* + + X. **Rekonsilasyun Dula (Reunion in Heaven),** *A Play, Irineo P. Goce (KaPule2 or Leonidas P. Agbayani)* + + XI. **Forgery of Rizal Retraction,** *Irineo P. Goce (KaPule2 or Leonidas P. Agbayani)* + + XII. **Maikling Kasaysayan Ng Malas Na Bayang Pilipinas,** *Ireneo P. Goce (KaPule2 or Leonidas P. Agbayani)*

Writings 5 Book - "Best Hopes" 2010, About President P-Noy + + I. **The Challenge of a Hundred Days: Believing that Filipinos can,** *Tony Meloto* + + II. **The 2006 Ramon Magsaysay Award for Community Service,** *for Tony Meloto* + + III. **Open Letter to Noynoy,** *F. Sionil Jose* + + IV. **A History of Pain,** *Juan L. Mercado* + + V. **An Open Letter to Noynoy,** *From OFWS* + + VI. **Pursuit of Good Governance Advocacies,** *Marcelo Tecson* + + VII. **A Fervent Prayer for Peace,** *Cesar Torres* + + VIII. **A History of Betrayal,** *Perry Diaz* + + IX. **Corona's Thorny Crown,** *Perry Diaz* + + X. **Dawn of a New Era,** *Perry Diaz* + + XI. **Of Mice, Boys and Men,** *Philip S. Chua, MD* + + XII. **A Hopeful Tomorrow - A Balikbayan Insight,** *Philip S. Chua, MD* + + XIII. **Global Filipinos: A Sleeping Giant,** *Philip S. Chua, MD* + + XIV. **Heart to Heart - Winds of Change,** *Philip S. Chua, MD* + + XV. **Growing Old is a Privilege,** *Philip S. Chua, MD* + + XVI. **Our Cruelty to Mother Earth,** *Philip S. Chua, MD* + + XVII. **Advice to Grads: "Never Choose Your Heroes Lightly",** *Ernie Delfin* + + XVIII. **Gawad Kalinga, A Progressive Movement,** *Ernie Delfin* + + XIX. **Why a Man Must Save and Invest,** *Ernie Delfin* + + XX. **Beautiful San Francisco, Pinoy Heaven,** *Ted Laguatan* + + XXI. **The next President and PAMUSA,** *Frank Wenceslao* + + XXII. **Philippne Budget Deficit,** *Frank Wenceslao* + + XXIII. **Money Laundering: US Tools vs. Corruption,** *Frank Wenceslao* + + XXIV. **Amid the Fighting, Clan Rules Maguindanao,** *Jaileen F. Jimeno* + + XXV. **Why I Publish Writings,** *Tatay Jobo Elizes* + + +

Writings 6 Book, 2010 + + I. SONA, State Of Nation Address, English, *Pres. Benigno Aquino III* + + II. SONA, State of Nation Address, Pilipino, *Pres. Benigno Aquino III* + + III. First 100 Days Speech, Pilipino, *Pres. Benigno Aquino III* + + IV. Finally, Another Ramon Magsaysay In The Making, *Bert Guiang.* + + V. A Covenant With Our President, *Tony Meloto* + + VI. From A Grateful Heart, A Thank You Letter, *Tony Meloto* + + VII. The Scent of Hope For The Global Filipino, *Tony Meloto* + + VIII. Fleshing Out The Broad Strokes, *Felicito (Tong) C. Payumo* + + IX. In Search Of Leaders (Part1), *Felicito (Tong) C. Payumo* + + X. In Search of Leaders (Part 2), *Felicito (Tong) C. Payumo* + + XI. A Conspiracy of Dunces, *Cesar Lumba* + + XII. Only Science Can Solve Poverty, *Flor Lacanilao* + + XIII. Education Reform Amid Scarcity, *Flor Lacanilao* + + XIV. Highblood: Obituaries/Reasons, *Flor Lacanilao* + + XV. How Money Works, *Edmund Lao* + XVI. State of Economy & Society, 2002, *Juan Dela Cruz (Txtmania)* + + XVII. Global Filipinos, *Juan Dela Cruz (Txtmania)* + + XVIII. Understanding Poverty, *Juan Dla Cruz (Txtmania)* + + XIX. Kuyakuy, *Dr. Ramon Marquez* + + XX. Cambodian Octopus, *Joey Jamito* + + XXI. Inspite Of Herself, I Still Love The Philippines, *Joey Jamito* + + XXII. Love Has Wings, *Percy Campoamor Cruz* + + XXIII. Walk For Kris, *Rod Garcia* + + XXIV. Coldblooded, But Alive, *Rod Garcia* + + XXV. It Takes A Village, *Rod Garcia* + + XXVI. Beauty Contest, *Rod Garcia* + + XXVII. Eight Points In Enlightening The Elites, *Orion Perez Dumdum* + + XXVIII. Case Against "Cellphone Revolution", *Sarah Raymundo*

Writings 7 Book, 2010 - My Vintage Pics (Biographical) Tatay Jobo Elizes

Writings 8 Book, 2010 + + I. The Church and the State: In Search of Common Ground, *Gel Santos Relos* + + II. President Aquino: "Walang Kaibigan, Walang Kamag-anak", *Gel Santos Relos* + + III. What Makes Us "Pinoy", *Gel Santos Relos* + + IV. Minsan May Isang Puta (2007), *Mike Portes* + + V. Build Our Dream, *Jose Ma. Montelibano* + + VI. Hope In Europe, *Tony Meloto* + + VII. Wealth in Canada, *Tony Meloto* + + VIII. Parenthood: A Sacred Covenant, *Philip S. Chua* + + IX. Are We, Humans, Really Civilize? (Or, are we for the birds.), *Philip S. Chua,* + + X. Save Our Nation, *Philip S. Chua* + + XI. A Time To Pause, *Philip S. Chua* + + XII. The Gawad Kalinga Virus, *Philip S. Chua* + + XIII. A Marching Order For P-Noy, *Philip S. Chua* + + XIV. "Bayan Ko" Bonds, *Philip S. Chua* + + XV. P-Noy's First 99 Days, *Philip S. Chua* + + XVI. The Practice of Quackery in the Phils, *Cesar D. Candari* + + XVII. Remember When? A Brief History of Old and Recent Past, *Cesar Candari* + + XVIII. The Philippines Before and What Now?, *Cesar D. Candari* + + XIX. The Traffic Problems are Beyond "Wang-Wang", *Cesar D. Candari* + + XX. Behind The Gold, *Eliseo Serina* + + XXI. May Angal? (Any Complaint?), *Greg B. Macabenta* + + XXII. Pagbalik-Tanaw Sa Kapatirang Masoneriya Sa Pilipina, *Irineo P. Goce* + + XXIII. Mysteries & Riddles Behind RP's Corridors Of Power, *Irineo P. Goce* + + XXIV. Wika - Diwa Ng Lahi, O, Ang Tore ni Babel Sa Pilipinas, *Irineo P. Goce* + + XXV. Can There Be Peace; Is There Hope For Progress?, *Irineo P. Coce* + + XXVI. Drama Queen, *Percival Campoamor Cruz* + + XXVII. Ang Tulay na Kahoy, *Percival Campoamor Cruz* + + XXVIII. Sa Alaala ni Maria Lorena Barros, *Percival Campoamor Cruz* + + XXIX. Text Game or Text Gambling?, *Juan dela Cruz* + + XXX. Of Husbands and Wives, *Juan dela Cruz* + + XXXI. It Must Be Love, *Juan dela Cruz* + + XXXII. Elite Triad Blocking Reform, *Demosthenes B. Donato*

Writings 9 Book, April 2011 + + I. Solidarity in Literature W/out Borders, *Simeon Dumdum Jr* + + II. Macario Sakay Vindicated, *Gemma Cruz Araneta* + + III. The Dilemma of the Last Filipino, *Larry Henares* + + IV. Ping Joaquin, Fil. Jazz Pianist, my Father, *Tony Joaquin* + + V. Bert Del Rosario, Inventor, Sing-Along, *Tony*

Olivares + + 13. **How US Can Create Jobs,** *Rob Ceralvo* + + 14. **Modus Operandi - Common Crimes (In Metro Manila, Philippines),** *Anonymous* + + 15. **Poem, Kabuhayang Bansa At Wika,** *Irineo P. Goce (aka KaPule 2 and Leonidas Agbayani)* + + 16. **Random Sayings & Advices,** *Anonymous*

Writings 12 Book, April 2012 + + 1. **Twenty Excuses Filipinos Use,** *Orion Perez Dumdum* + + 2. **One By One, The Petals Drop,** *Julia C. Lagoc* + + 3. **Religion & the Scientist,** *Honorio M. Cruz, MD* + + 4. **The Tales of the Aswang & Bangungot,** *Honorio M. Cruz, MD* + + 5. **Sex & Politics,** *Honrio M. Cruz, MD* + + 6. **Autopsy,** *Ben Gonzales, MD* + + 7. **Geekmocracy,** *Mar-Vic Cagurangan* + + 8. **Flights: Voice from the Future that Lives in the Past,** *Mar-Vic Cagurangan* + + 9. **Kaya Natin! Sanctuary,** *Marisa Lerias* + + 10. **The Days of Courage,** *Gerry Partido* + + 11. **Earth Day and the Tragedy of a Famous River,** *Cesar D. Candari, MD, FCAP Emeritus* + + 12. **Few Filipino-American Nonprofits Getting Political,** *Erwin De Leon* + + 13. **Filipino-American Political Invisibility And Community Organizations,** *Erwin De Leon* I+ + 14. **I'm 32 and I am still a Virgin,** *Jovelyn Bayubay Revilla* + + 15. **Hiding Ill-Gotten Wealth,** *Jobo Elizes*

Solo Authored Books: + + +

Book A, **Turning Points - Empty Dreams,** *Job Elizes Sr,1968 (Reissue 2009)* + +
Book B, **Be Considerate - Behaviour Issues,** *Tatay Jobo Elizes (Jr), 2009* + + +
Book C, **Piglets Unlimited - Wealth Untapped,** *Tatay Jobo Elizes, 2009* + +
Book D, **Out of the Misty Sea We Must,** *Cesar Lumba, 2010* + + +
Book E, **Fulfilled** - *Gonzales Reynaldo, Editor, 2010* + + +

Book F, **Reflections** - *Bert Guiang, 2010* + + +
Book G, **Writings 7 - My Vintage Pics,** *Tatay Jobo Elizes, 2010* + + +
Book H, **May Bagwis Ang Pag-ibig,** *Percival C. Cruz* + + +
Book I, **Letters To Matrimony,** *Irineo Perez Coce, Ka Pule2, 2011* + + +
Book J, **Songs I Wish You Knew,** *Soledad R. Juan, 2011* + + +

Book K, **Make My Day,** *Larry Henares Jr., 1993, Re-issue 2011* + + +
Book L, **Our Guerrero Family,** *Tatay Jobo Elizes, 2010* + + +
Book M, **Jokes Collection,** *Tatay Jobo Elizes, 2011* +
Book N, **FaveArt 1,** *Tatay Jobo Elizes, 2011* + +
Book O, **Beyond idle thoughts,** *MLMunoz, Sept,2011* + + +

Book P, **Cracks In The Armor,** *Mariano Ngan, Oct 2011* + + +
Book Q, **FaveArt 2,** *Tatay Jobo Elizes, 2011* + +
Book R, **Balitang Kutsero,** *Perry Diaz, Jan 2012* + + +
Book S, **FaveArt3,** *Tatay Jobo, 2011* + + +
Book T, **FaveArt4** *,2012, Tatay Jobo* + + +

Book U, **Stack Family Journals,** *Phil & Fe Stack, 2012* + + +
Book V, **Emily, An Adoption Journey,** *Romerl Elizes, 2012* + + +
Book W, **Hermes Alegre Art Gallery,** *TJ & Hermes, 2012* + + +
Book X**, Masaya Din, Malungkot Din,** *Jovelyn Bayubay Revilla, 2012* + + +
Book Y, **Tiis, Sipag At Tiyaga,** *Raquel Delfin Padilla, 2012* + + +

Book Z, **Until I Meet You,** *Jhackie Eslit Bayobay,* **2012** + + +
Book AA, **Buhay At Pag-ibig,** *Argel Lucero Tamayo, 2012* + + +
Book AB, **Hail to the Second Best,** *Dr. Philip Stack, 2012* + + +
Book AC, **Life Bus,** *Mommy Joyce Pineda-Faulmino, 2012* + + +
Book AD, **My Candid Musings,** *Monette Dioquino Calugay, 2012* + + +

Book AE, **Tickets to Life,** *Maria Lourdes Jesalva, 2012* + + +
Book AF, **The Dove Files,** *Mike Portes, 2012* + +
Book AG, **Nursing Vignettes,** *Jocelyn Cerrudo Sese, 2012* + + +
Book AH, **Poor Ba Us,** *R.A. Gubalane, 2012* + +
Book AI, **Summer Idyll,** *Avelina Gil, 2012* + +

Book AJ, **Legacy (Pamana),** *Rachel Astrero, 2012* + + +
Book AK, **Narratives Old & New,** *Avelina J. Gil, 2013* + + +
Book AL, **Buhay Saudi,** *Adelle J. Esic, 2013* + + +
Book AM, **Buhay OFW atbp,** *Jessica Napat, 2013* + + +
Book AN, **Mga Tula Ng Buhay,** *Angelita C.Esguerra, 2013* + + +

Book AO, **Not By Bread Alone,** *Judge Lily Vidallon-Magtolis, 2013* + + +

Please buy online at www.amazon.com *or* www.createspace.com *or give as gift in hard copy or kindle edition, if applicable. All authors and titles are easy to search, trace or find online. Thanks. Self--Publisher Tatay Jobo Elizes*

www.ingramcontent.com/pod-product-compliance
Lightning Source LLC
Chambersburg PA
CBHW070546290526
45790CB00002B/597